Games for Football Training

To make its mark in even a junior soccer championship today a team must be supremely fit, with speed both on and off the ball and capable of fast reflexes in tight situations. The 157 games described in these pages will promote all these needs as well as make training a stimulating experience.

The work-outs, covering goalkeeping, passing, shooting, heading, tackling, dribbling and all aspects of ball control, as well as stamina building, are presented in clearly understood terms and amplified by explicit line drawings. Rules of each game, duration, suggested variations and aim of the exercise are tabulated for easy assimilation by readers at all levels.

As Sir Stanley Rous comments in his Foreword, the first essential for building sound footballers is to start with boys who easily acquire correct muscular habits and quick co-ordination of brain and body; *Games for Football Training* is carefully graduated to meet the physical standards of all players from schoolboys up and becomes required reading for every soccer coach and a must for every sportsmaster's library.

Graham Ross.

Games for Football Training

**Günter Lammich and
Dr Heinz Kadow**

Nelson

Thomas Nelson and Sons Ltd
36 Park Street London W1Y 4DE

Nelson (Africa) Ltd
PO Box 18123 Nairobi Kenya

Thomas Nelson (Australia) Ltd
171–175 Bank Street South Melbourne
Victoria 3205

Thomas Nelson and Sons (Canada) Ltd
81 Curlew Drive Don Mills Ontario

Thomas Nelson (Nigeria) Ltd
PO Box 336 Apapa Lagos

First published in 1970 in East Germany

First published in Great Britain by Thomas Nelson and Sons Ltd, 1974

Copyright © 1966 by Sportverlag Berlin

Translated from the German by Robin and Hella Oliver

Edited by A. R. Mills

Illustrations by Klaus Zühl

All Rights Reserved. No part of this publication may be reproduced, stored in a retrieval system, or transmitted, in any form or by any means, electronic, mechanical, photocopying, recording or otherwise, without the prior permission of the publishers.

ISBN 0 17 149060 6
Filmset and printed by Thomson Litho, East Kilbride, Scotland

Contents

Foreword	7
Introduction	9
Games and competitions for warming up	15
Games for improving physical fitness	33
Skill-training games	71
Games for tactical training	145
Supplementary games	177

Foreword

by Sir Stanley Rous, C.B.E.

Many soccer players go about their game in a surprisingly casual way. The enjoyment and excitement are all that matter and coaching and preparation are often considered tedious and irksome, but under the direction of a skilled coach who introduces a scientific approach getting fit can be fun, and not only does the player perform better because he is fitter, but he soon realises that good training is the best insurance against injury.

Coaches must remember, however, that young players quickly tire of a monotonous repetition of mechanical exercises and should always be on the alert to switch from one type of activity to another. In *Games For Football Training* they will find plenty of material to enable them to do just that. I have seen many of the preliminary practices and minor games described in these pages employed with great success by coaches throughout the world; here they are arranged so progressively and are so well illustrated that they will help a coach to prepare his work thoroughly and ensure that his pupils, whether outdoors or indoors, learn through small games the skills required in soccer. The first essential for building sound footballers is to start with boys who easily acquire correct muscular habits and quick coordination of brain and body. It is from their ranks that the senior players for the professional and amateur clubs will be found, and it is this sort of book which will help to produce them.

STANLEY ROUS

Introduction

The instructions and rules are easy to understand throughout the book but the following points should be noted:

1. Every game has its own competitive scoring system. Generally the winner is the scorer of more goals than the opponent.
   In every form of competition the better or faster team is the winner. Only in the technique-improvement games is there a "moral" victor, i.e. it is the "better" team who is in possession of the ball, while the others have to make a tackle or an interception in order to stay in the game.
2. All the F.A. rules which cover such points as players' kit, unlawful play or unsporting behaviour, as well as kick-offs, goal-kicks, free-kicks, corners, penalties, throw-ins or off-sides, apply throughout.
3. Those rules which are often altered, i.e. applying to areas and boundaries, duration of play or number of players, are redefined for the description of each game and the main points explained.
4. Any departure from the normal rules is specially mentioned. The illustration featured with each game depicts its essential idea, but for obvious reasons is not always in proportion.

For reasons of clarity the games have been numbered consecutively and classified according to their main features:

No. 1–18: Games and competitions for warming-up
These are characterised by their full use of bodily movement, and in conjunction with gymnastic exercises are best suited for the acceleration of the muscular warming-up process.

These games are both intensive and uninterrupted. It is therefore necessary to pay attention that no excessive strain should be placed on the physical capabilities of the players. Given their light-hearted nature, they are more suited to the players' amusement than to satisfying competitive instincts. It should be noted that though they are position-changing exercises, games 12–18 have been put into this group due to their value as warm-up routines.

No. 19–53: Games for improving physical fitness
Fitness is here taken to mean a certain stage of development or stamina, speed and strength. The games are listed in that order. In the description of the games and the remarks following them the

results of research into training methods has been taken into account as far as possible. The main basis is the methodical use of stamina training, interval training and pressure training, and it must be stressed that the degree of severity of the training should be adapted to the physical capacities of the players. Particularly important in this respect is the length of the intervals. In order to give the body the correct incentive to exert itself it must be trained to the point of tiredness, so that the intervals should afford respite but not complete physical recovery.

For the speed-training games it's obviously sensible to introduce longer intervals and greater recuperation, since in this way the incentive for short, intensive bursts is created.

The decisive factor in these games which build up certain muscles is that those muscles not being used in the actual exercise be employed during the interval while relaxing the others. Since the strength routines are particularly strenuous it is important for their effectiveness that the correct dosage of training is given.

No. 54–122: Skill-training games

Training particular skills by means of competitive games has the advantage that all rehearsed moves must be carried out at a realistic pace and under conditions resembling a real match. It is, however, necessary that the players concerned have already mastered the basics of soccer technique. These games are unsuitable for initial teaching, since beginners can easily acquire false ideas which once ingrained become very difficult to correct afterwards.

Since these games place great onus on footballing ability, and exceed the demands made by a simple game of football, multiple skills can be acquired and players are able to develop their ability to improvise on their personal styles. For these reasons the games are extremely valuable and of greater use than a host of simpler coaching routines.

The physical strain imposed by the games also creates the necessity to use the acquired skills correctly at speed, and so to perfect them. Trainers should pay particular attention to the use of both feet during these activities.

No. 123–151: Games for tactical training

These games, which train individual as well as team skills, require a certain alertness on the part of the players. It is usually advisable to break off during a game if a tactical error has been committed and give corrective help. Individual talents, improvisation and unforeseen moves should not be repressed, i.e. basic training and intuition should be on a level footing in these training exercises.

No. 152–157: Supplementary games

Whereas all the previous games relate to footballing skills, this section incorporates other sports. They have an important place in football training for loosening-up. The rules have been partly simplified or adapted to the F.A. rules in order to make their explanation easier. In addition to their value for warming-up they all have an importance in a player's overall training and, of course, serve to improve general fitness.

These 157 games for football training are designed primarily to give a spur to creative effort in training. They make no claim to completeness and coaches and players can try to add to the collection with their own ideas.

Games and competitions for warming-up

1   'Soccer Marbles'

Purpose:	Warm-up routine.
No. of players:	3 players to a group.
Playing area:	Any size, up to full pitch.
Duration:	20 mins. maximum.
Outline:	2 players try to rob the dribbler as often as possible by kicking their balls against his ball.
Rules:	Each player has a ball. One in each group dribbles his ball up and down the field. The other two try to knock the dribbler's ball away from his feet. A player may kick only his own ball. If a shot misses, the player must retrieve the ball himself. If he "scores", he changes places with the dribbler.
Possible variation:	Specify the method used to dribble or shoot, i.e. left foot or right.
Remarks:	For schoolboys or beginners it's worthwhile restricting the area to avoid unnecessary running.

2 Crossing the Pitch with Ball

Purpose:	Warm-up routine.
No. of players:	No limit.
Playing area:	Section of pitch 30–60m. wide.
Duration:	15–20 mins.
Outline:	Rapid dribbling of ball across to opposite touch-line. The team whose balls all finish on the opposite line first, wins one point.
Rules:	The players are split into two teams and stand on opposite touchlines. Each player has a ball. On the word go each player dribbles to the other touchline.
Possible variations:	1. Start from other points on the pitch. 2. It's a good idea to do forward rolls, sit-ups, cartwheels etc. before this exercise. Twists and jumps can be introduced into the dribbling routine.
Remarks:	Care should be taken that the two opposing teams don't obstruct each other as they cross.

3   Passing among Teams

Purpose:	Warm-up routine.
No. of players:	2 teams of 5–8 players.
Playing area:	Penalty box.
Duration:	20 mins. maximum.
Outline:	Each player passes the ball accurately to his teammate, errors in play losing points.
Rules:	Both teams have their own ball, each marked differently. Points are lost if a player passes to a member of the other team, or if the ball goes out of play. After each mistake the sequence is restarted from the point where the error occurred. Points are also lost if the ball is passed directly back to the previous player without a third man having touched it. Two umpires are needed for this game to follow each of the two balls and to keep score of the points.
Possible variation:	Limit the number of times one player may play the ball, or even permit direct passes only.
Remarks:	Adjust the size of pitch to the players' capabilities. The smaller the area, the more difficult it is to pass the ball among the team members.

4   Moving Targets

Purpose:	Warm-up routine.
No. of players:	2 teams of 6–8 players.
Playing area:	Penalty box extended sideways to touchlines.
Duration:	Up to 20 mins.
Outline:	One team tries to score points by hitting an opponent with the ball without losing possession. The other team tries to gain possession. One point for every opponent hit.
Rules:	Both teams are on the pitch together. Direct passing only. Dribbling is not permitted. The opposing team gets the ball after every shot missed, if the ball goes out of play, if an opposing player gets the ball first from a throw-in or if a player goes over the boundary line. A player hit rejoins the game only if one of his team-mates regains the ball.
Possible variation:	Players hit drop out, the game ending when no more players are left on one side. The last player of a team is allowed to dribble the ball.
Remarks:	This exercise is particularly suitable for indoor practice.

5 'Piggy in the Middle'

Purpose:	Warm-up routine.
No. of players:	4 against 1, 6 against 2, 8 against 3.
Playing area:	Max. 20m. × 20m.
Duration:	20 mins. maximum.
Outline:	"Piggy" tries to intercept the ball being passed among members of the team.
Rules:	If the player in the middle intercepts, he changes places with the man who last played the ball. The ball is also lost if it goes out of play. In this case, the player at fault changes places with the player who has been in the middle longest. Passes may be done on the ground or in the air. Handling is not allowed.
Possible variation:	Limit the number of times the ball can be played or permit direct passes only. It is possible to play this game with two balls, but anyone passing one ball to a player who already has the other ball becomes "piggy".
Remarks:	Adjust the size of pitch and number of players to the standard of the players.

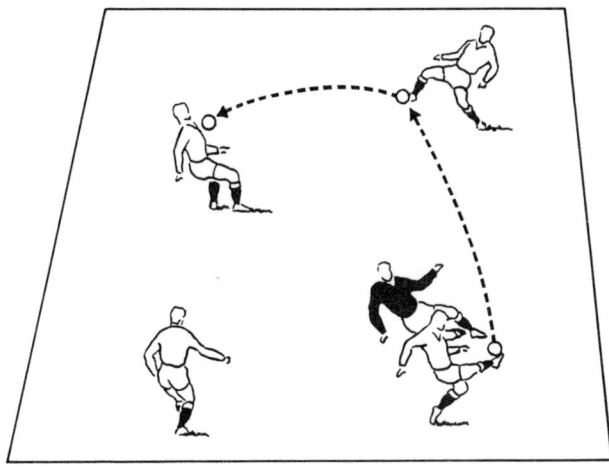

6   Bulldog

Purpose: Warm-up routine.
No. of players: 10–20.
Playing area: Crosswise in one half of the pitch.
Duration: 20 mins. maximum.
Outline: Two players, passing the ball to each other, try to hit another player beneath the waist with the ball. Any player hit joins the attackers. The game ends when only one player remains "free". He and another player of his choice then re-start the game.
Rules: The attackers must pass. Dribbling is not allowed. To distinguish the two sides it's usually necessary for them to wear different coloured shirts. For example, those with similarly coloured jerseys should begin as the side without the ball, and remove their jerseys as they are captured by the other side. Any player who runs over the boundary lines is counted as captured.
Possible variation: The entire body can be used as the target area.
Remarks: This game is suitable for playing in the gymnasium, when the wallbars can be used as cushions.

7   All against All

Purpose:	Warm-up routine.
No. of players:	10–20.
Playing area:	Penalty box extended to sidelines, divided into two halves by a middle line.
Duration:	20 mins. maximum.
Outline:	A ball is thrown in; whoever gets it first can "shoot" at any other player. There are no teams. The last player remaining is the winner.
Rules:	All players in one half of the area. The referee throws the ball in. Anyone who is hit drops out, as does anyone who shoots and misses. After a hit, the player who gets the ball first from the rebound plays on; likewise when the ball goes out of play.
Possible variation:	The eliminated players begin another game in the other half of the area.
Remarks:	For the second game it is useful to have a second referee.

8   Team Tag

Purpose:	Warm-up routine.
No. of players:	3 teams each of 2–5 players.
Playing area:	Penalty area extended to sidelines.
Duration:	20 mins. maximum.
Outline:	Each player has a ball. One team tries to score by tagging members of the other two teams. Anyone tagged must drop out and squat down on the sidelines.
Rules:	Tagging is done by touching with the hands; a player is also "had" if he loses control of his ball and/or crosses the boundary. These players go to the edge of the area and squat down. They can be released by their team-mates touching them. If one team succeeds in tagging all the other players, then another team becomes tag. The game ends when all the teams have been tag.
Possible variations:	1. Whoever is tagged lies down on the sideline, making his release more difficult for his team-mates. 2. In setting a team-mate free, only the ball may be touched.
Remarks:	Suitable for gymnasium or outside.

9   Circular Tag

Purpose:	Warm-up routine.
No. of players:	8–12.
Playing area:	All players form a circle, standing about 2–3 yards apart.
Duration:	15 mins. maximum.
Outline:	Players stand with legs wide apart. One player is "tag", one other the "victim". Both have a ball. If the victim is caught, these two players change places. If the victim manages to play the ball through the legs of one of the other players and crawl through after it before he is caught, he then plays the ball to another player, who in turn becomes the "victim".
Rules:	The pursuit takes place only around the outside of the circle. Tagging is done only with the hand. If the victim loses control of the ball or kicks it into the circle, he then becomes "tag".
Possible variations:	1. Rolling the ball with the hand (instead of dribbling). 2. Dribbling or rolling the ball with the left or right foot or hand only.
Remarks:	The size of circle should be small enough to allow the tag a chance of catching the other man.

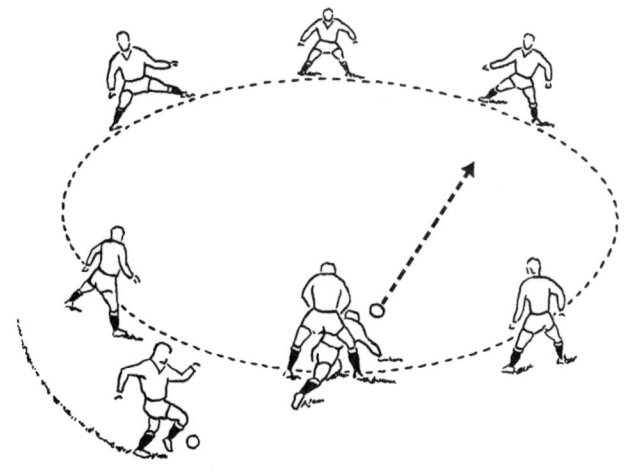

10   Team Tennis

Purpose:	Warm-up routine.
No. of players:	7 maximum.
Playing area:	20 × 10m., with a net across the middle of the area.
Duration:	20–30 mins. or up to a score of ten points.
Outline:	The ball is kicked back and forth across the net. Each player tries to reach the ball and return it in such a way that the next man is unable to retrieve it, and is so forced to drop out. When this happens the last two men to have played the ball are given one point.
Rules:	The players line up on the base lines, the same number at either end. One player kicks or knees the ball over the net and runs clockwise round the playing area and takes up position as last in the row of players at the other end. The ball he has kicked is returned, after it has bounced, by the first in line, who in turn runs to the other end. Any player who does not reach the ball or miskicks, drops out.
Possible variation:	The game can be made more demanding if the players are made to perform exercises while changing ends, e.g. sit-ups, press-ups, squat jumps etc., or are made to leap the net instead of just running round it.

11   Lofted Passing in Sequence

Purpose:	Warm-up routine.
No. of players:	9 maximum.
Playing area:	25 × 25m.
Duration:	20–25 mins. or up to a score of 5 points.
Outline:	The ball played by one player is to be retrieved and played by the next, the idea being to make it as difficult as possible for him to reach the ball, and to force him into losing a point. The two players left in each round are awarded one point. First to five is overall winner.
Rules:	Players are numbered. No. 1 begins by kicking the ball into the air; No. 2 must play next, the ball not being allowed to bounce more than once. Players are eliminated if the ball is touched more than once consecutively by the same player; or if the ball does not go above head-height, is kicked directly to touch, or if a player is unable to reach the ball in time. Eliminated players sit the round out and perform exercises (skipping, exercises on the bar).
Possible variations:	1. Introduce additional exercises after each man has played the ball (head-rolls, jumps etc.). 2. Ball to be played with one foot only (specify which):

12 Changing Positions in Circle

Purpose: Warm-up routine.
No. of players: 4–10.
Playing area: Circular, diameter 10 × 20m.
Duration: 15–20 mins.
Outline: A player, having played the ball, takes up a new position and remains there until he receives the ball again. The competitive element lies in that the ball must be passed a minimum number of times. Two circles can compete against each other.
Rules: The players stand in a circle. The ball is passed to any other player, the passer of the ball moving to the position of the player to whom he has passed the ball: the receiver then passes the ball on and follows it to his new position, and so on. The players must be prevented from obstructing one another.
Possible variations: 1. Vary the mode of passing the ball (direct passing, with trapping, row passes, knee-high, one bounce etc.).
2. Ball to be headed instead of passed (reduce diameter of circle).
3. Introduce a second ball.

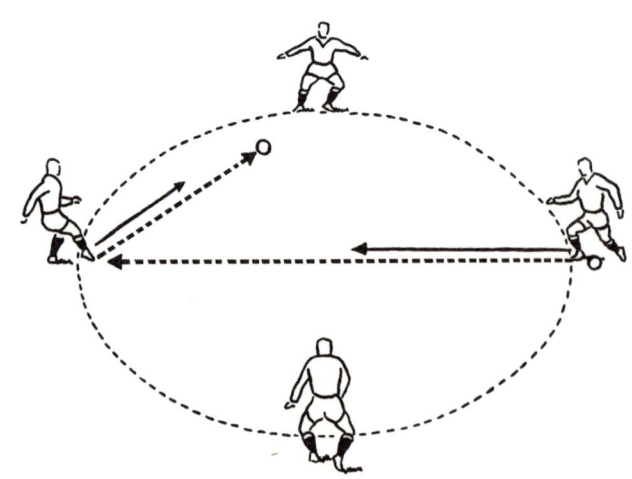

13   Changing Positions—Triangular

Purpose:	Warm-up routine.
No. of players:	3.
Playing area:	Triangular, sides 10–20m. long.
Duration:	10–15 mins.
Outline:	Rapid changing of position after passing the ball. The game can be made competitive either by playing against the clock or against other teams of three.
Rules:	Players stand at the corners of a triangle which has already been marked out. Player No. 1 passes the ball to player No. 2, but changes places with player No. 3. The player with the ball passes it on to another player, changing over with the "free" man.
Possible variation:	Method of passing to be stipulated. After some practice it should become possible to abandon the marked triangle and continue the game anywhere without loss of fluency, thereby saving space.
Remarks:	At first, this exercise needs considerable concentration. It is best to begin slowly and methodically, paying particular attention to the marked lines.

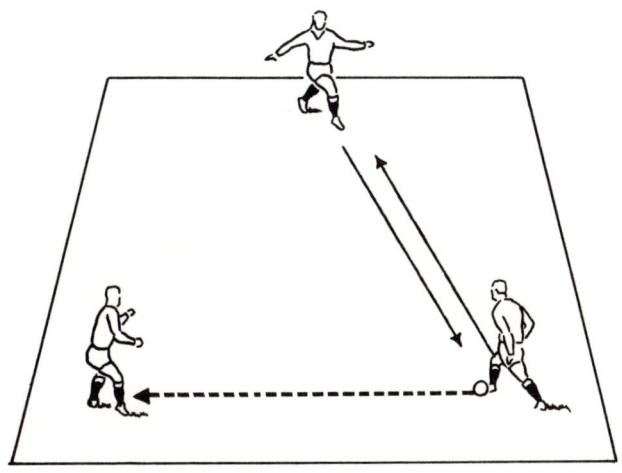

14 Changing Positions—Rectangular

Purpose:	Warm-up routine.
No. of players:	4.
Playing area:	Rectangle, 5–20m. × 10–30m.
Duration:	15–20 mins.
Outline:	Rapid place-changing plus accurate passing.
Rules:	Players stand on corners of marked rectangle. The first player plays the ball along the longer side of the area to the next man, and runs after it. The second player plays the ball *diagonally* across the rectangle, but runs back to the free position, i.e. from where player No. 1 started. On the opposite side of the rectangle the other two players do the same, so that only the ball crosses the area, the players changing their position in pairs.
Possible variations:	1. Direction of passes may be changed, so that, on the whistle, players change places along the short sides of the rectangle. 2. It is possible to get the players to do exercises while changing places, e.g. rabbit hops, shoulder rolls, hopping on alternate feet etc.
Remarks:	At first, this exercise needs considerable concentration. It is best to begin slowly and methodically, paying particular attention to the marked lines.

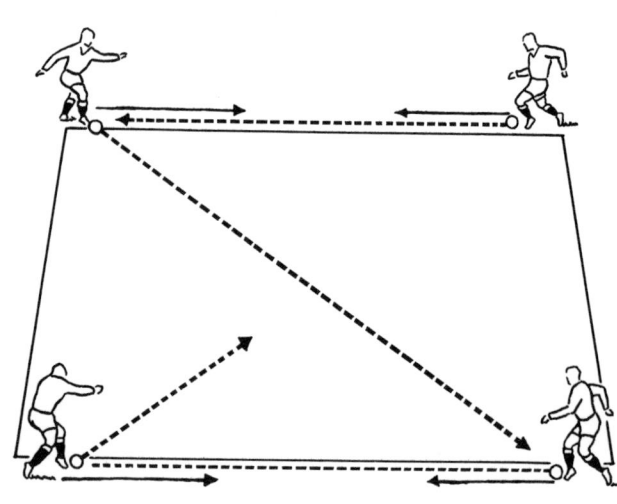

15   Changing Position—Crosswise

Purpose:	Warm-up routine.
No. of players:	Any number, 3 to a team.
Playing area:	Length of area dependent on number of teams. Width 25–50m.
Duration:	15 to 25 mins.
Outline:	The ball should be passed from one side of the area to the other, the player sprinting across to the other side. Winner is the team who completes the greatest number of changes within the time allowed.
Rules:	One player stands across the pitch from the two others of his team, who have the ball. One of these two passes the ball across to his team-mate and sprints after it; the receiver passes the ball back to the third man, and likewise sprints across. A constant changing of position is thus achieved.
Possible variations:	1. Vary the kind of pass, and the technique employed. 2. Various exercises, e.g. knee-bends, sit-ups, backward or forward rolls, can be added after each player has passed the ball.
Remark:	Ensure that any additional exercises are compatible with the amount of sprinting required.

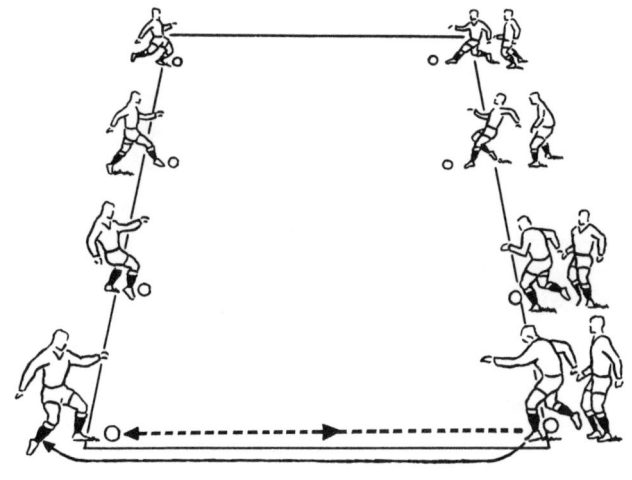

16 Changing Position—Relay

Purpose:	Warm-up routine.
No. of players:	8.
Playing area:	30 × 5m.
Duration:	15–20 mins.
Outline:	Quick return of pass, with rapid changing of position.
Rules:	Players are divided into two teams of four which take up position in two single files, facing one another some 30m. apart. The first player passes the ball to the front player of the opposite line, runs in the same direction, but goes to the back of the line. The ball receiver runs on to the pass, returning it immediately to the opposite side, and runs round to the back of the line, and so on.
Possible variations:	1. Stipulate method of passing to be used. 2. Erect a small goal between the two lines, each player to kick the ball through the goal. 3. The player who passes can also act as a non-challenging defender. 4. Passing done with the head.
Remarks:	"Accuracy before speed." Concentrate on accuracy first in any competition between groups.

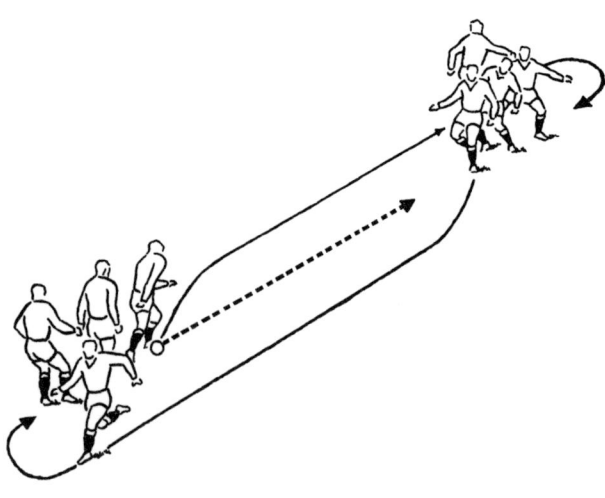

17   Changing Position in Groups of 3

Purpose:	Warm-up routine.
No. of players:	Any number: 3 players to a team.
Playing area:	20 × 20m.
Duration:	20 mins. maximum.
Outline:	Rapid switch of position in reaching a pass. Winning team is the one which switches the greatest number of times.
Rules:	The players stand in triangular formation, the same distance from one another. One man passes the ball to either of the others, but stays where he is. The player at whom the pass is aimed does not take it but runs to the position of the third player, who in turn runs across to receive the pass. He in turn passes to either of the others, but himself stays still, and so on.
Possible variations:	1. Fix method of passing, left or right foot. 2. Place small obstacles along the sides of the triangle (hurdles, medicine balls etc.) over which players must chip the ball and jump.
Remarks:	Begin routine slowly and then gradually introduce competition. This exercise is very strenuous, so allow a pause every 5 mins. for practising easier techniques.

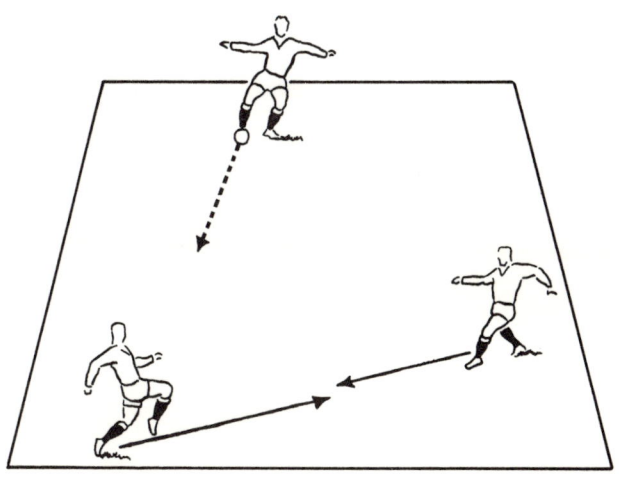

18   Changing Positions—Circular with Pivot

Purpose: Warm-up routine.
No. of players: Any number, 7 players per circle.
Playing area: Circle, diameter 15–25m.
Duration: 20 mins. maximum.
Outline: Rapid passing and moving into a free position. Competition either as contest between several groups—which group can switch over the most often—or individually by deducting points based on the number of passing and running errors made by each individual player.
Rules: Six players stand round the circle, with the seventh player in the middle with the ball. He passes the ball to one of the players on the circumference but runs to the place of another player, who must then leave his place and run to the middle of the circle. The player who has been passed the ball returns the pass to the middle, and the process repeats itself.
Possible variation: Change places by calling out names.
Remarks: Practise slowly at first, then play competitively. Trapping and holding the ball makes the exercise easier.

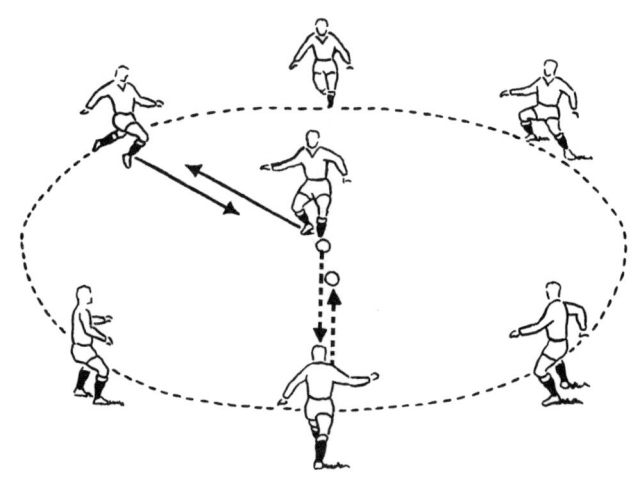

Games for improving physical fitness

19   Midfield Build-Up

Purpose:	Stamina training.
No. of players:	2 teams of 4 players.
Playing area:	30 × 20m., two small-size goals on the sidelines, the goalmouths facing outwards from the pitch.
Duration:	Maximum 10 × 5 mins., with pauses.
Outline:	Two players of one team must work the ball out of their own half into an attacking position, so as to be able to pass the ball to their team-mates who will be positioned in front of the opposing goal; he in turn is marked by one of the opposition. If the ball is lost the other team continues the game by attacking.
Rules:	A goal may be scored only after a pass from within the opposing half. The two in-field players may not cross the boundary lines. Passes from within that team's own half are reckoned as faults and are penalised by a free-kick. The two mid-field players change over with those standing in front of the goals every 5 minutes.
Possible variations:	1. The length of pitch, length of intervals or number of passes allowed can be altered to suit the capabilities of the players. 2. Mid-field players may be changed after each goal scored.

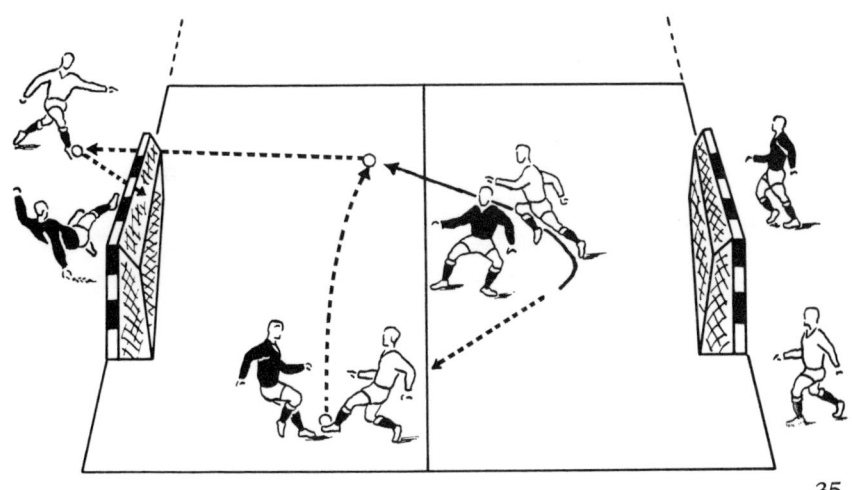

Midfield Fitness

Purpose:	Stamina training.
No. of players:	2 teams of 5.
Playing area:	Lengthwise, including penalty areas.
Duration:	Maximum 6 × 5 mins., with short intervals.
Outline:	The players of each line are positioned as follows: 2 in own penalty area; 2 in midfield; 1 in opposing penalty area. The two players in midfield each win one point if they succeed in reaching their own player in the opposing penalty box with a pass.
Rules:	The game begins with the defence in their own penalty area. They evade the one opponent and pass the ball out to their players in midfield. Here there are two against two, and a point is awarded when the ball is successfully passed into the penalty area. If the other side win the ball, play continues without a break.
Possible variations:	1. Midfield players to be changed every 5 mins. 2. A point may also be awarded if the attacking player is able to return the ball to midfield.
Remarks:	The game is simplified if one "defender" is removed.

21   Two against two in the Corner

Purpose: Stamina training.
No. of players: 2 teams of 4.
Playing area: Corner of pitch, about 15 × 15m.
Duration: 1 min. on, 1 min. interval.
Outline: Team has to dribble the ball over the opponents' line to score. The winner is the team with the most "goals" after a given length of time.
Rules: Only two players are on at any time. Players are changed at one-minute intervals. One team starts off by mounting the attack on the opposition goal-line. The skill lies in building up an attacking position which enables the ball to be easily controlled and taken over the opponents' goal-line. A goal is scored each time the ball is *dribbled* over the line.
Possible variation: Extend the time "on" to 2 mins. Time "off" must also be extended equivalently, and can be used for simple skills practice.
Remarks: This routine is particularly suitable for more proficient players.

22   Three against Three in Penalty Area

Purpose:	Stamina training.
No. of players:	2 teams of 6.
Playing area:	Penalty area.
Duration:	5 × 2 mins. of exercise, 2 mins. rest in between.
Outline:	A team must get the ball across the opponents' goal-line to score. The winner is the team with the highest score after a given time.
Rules:	Only 3 players of each team on at any time. Players are changed every 2 mins. One team starts by mounting an attack on the opponents' goal-line. The skill lies in building up an attacking position so as to enable the ball to be easily controlled and taken over the goal-line. No offside rule.
Possible variation:	Players changed every 3 mins.
Remarks:	The intervals can be utilised for skill-routines.

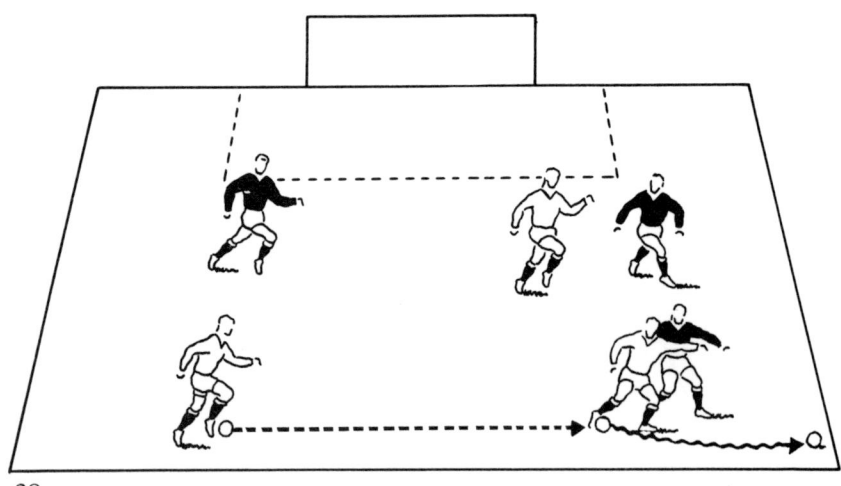

23 Handicap-Football

Purpose:	Stamina training.
No. of players:	8 players, 5 *v.* 3.
Playing area:	30 × 30m.
Duration:	Maximum 6 × 5 mins., short intervals between periods.
Outline:	Teams attempt to retain possession of ball as long as possible. One minute scores one point. The winner is the team with most points after a given time.
Rules:	One team passes the ball around. The opponents try to gain possession. The team of 5 players have a handicap—first-time passing—whereas the team of 3 are allowed all legal means. When one team gains a point, they can opt either to continue or to give the ball to the other side.
Possible variations:	1. Team of 5 allowed only along-the-ground passing, or only left-foot passing etc. 2. After 5 mins. players are changed round.
Remarks:	Adapt the game to the capabilities of the players.

24   Change-of-Ends Game

Purpose:	Stamina training.
No. of players:	8–12. Minimum 4 against 4, Maximum 6 against 6.
Playing area:	Both halves of a football pitch, the half-way line marked exactly, two hockey-sized goals.
Duration:	60 mins. maximum.
Outline:	One team attacks, the other defending their own goal. The attacking side retains possession and may continue straight after a goal has been scored, but the game then switches round and they attack the goal at the other end.
Rules:	A goal is allowed only when all members of the attack are in their opponent's half. If one team loses the ball, the other team become the attackers. The team in possession retains possession of the ball only if they succeed in scoring, continuing the game by attacking the goal at the far end. No goalkeepers. No handling. No offside rules.
Possible variation:	The game can be made suitable for all ages and standards.

25 Breaking Through

Purpose:	Stamina training.
No. of players:	4–6. One goalkeeper and at least 3 but at most 5 other players.
Playing area:	One half of the pitch including the goal.
Duration:	40 mins. max. 5-minute periods with 3-minute intervals for simple exercises of skill.
Outline:	All against all. As soon as one player has the ball, all others are against him. He attempts to break through and score a goal.
Rules:	Play is started by a goal-kick. The game continues if any player is robbed of the ball by any other, the first man then becoming part of the defence. Play is restarted by the goalkeeper after balls out of play or goals scored.
Possible variations:	1. Both the goals may be used by different groups. 2. Teams are reformed after each 5-minute period, the best player of one group being pitted against the best of the other group.
Remarks:	Adapt the length and strenuousness of the game to ability of players.

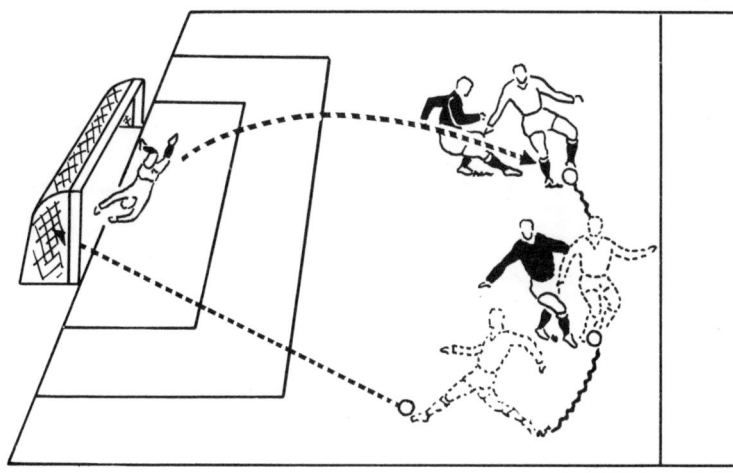

26 Small-Pitch Soccer with Hurdles as Goals

Purpose:	Stamina training.
No. of players:	2 teams of 5–7 players.
Playing area:	Between half-way line and edge of penalty box extended outwards, with two hurdles placed 3m. behind the "goal-lines".
Duration:	4–6 × 5 mins.
Outline:	Teams attack their opponents half trying to score goals.
Rules:	No goalkeeper or offside rule. A goal is scored when the ball is kicked through the hurdle. The boundary lines must not be crossed either by attackers or defenders. In this case a free kick is given at the point of infringement.
Possible variation:	After each 5-minute session, a pause of 2–3 minutes may be occupied by technique drills.
Remarks:	The distance between the hurdles and the goal-lines may be varied.

27   **Fitness Training with two Hockey Goals**

Purpose: Stamina training.
No. of players: 3 teams of 3.
Playing area: Both halves of pitch, two hockey-size goals, 2 extra balls.
Duration: 3 × maximum 15 mins. per team.
Outline: One team attacks both goals alternately, scoring as many goals as possible, the two other teams acting as defences. After each team has completed its run, the goals are reckoned up and the winner announced.
Rules: The attacking team attempts to score as many goals as possible in the 15 mins. The number of attacks feasible depends on the amount of running the team can manage. If the ball is lost to the defence, the attack regains it immediately but play reverses direction. If a shot at goal misses, one of the extra balls is rolled into play so that the game can continue. No offside, corners or in touch.
Possible variations: 1. The length of the attacking period can be varied according to the strength of the team in possession.
2. Teams need not be of equal strength.
Remarks: The balls off the pitch are fetched by the "free" defending team.
The strenuousness of the exercise should be matched to the fitness of the players.

28 All up in Attack

Purpose:	Stamina training.
No of players:	2 teams of 3–6 players.
Playing area:	One half of pitch with half-way line well marked; two hockey-size goals.
Duration:	90 mins. maximum.
Outline:	All members of the attacking team must have left their own half and be in the opposing half before a goal may be scored. The other team defends, trying to win the ball.
Rules:	A goal counts only when all attacking players are in the opposition's half. The other side is given the ball if this is not the case when:
	(**a**) a shot is made at the goal;
	(**b**) if they intercept a pass;
	(**c**) after fouls;
	(**d**) the ball goes out of play.
	No proper goalkeepers. The last player of each team may handle the ball as the ultimate defence. No offside rule.
Possible variations:	1. Teams of 7 or over to use full-size pitch.
	2. If goalkeepers are used, they alone may remain in their own half throughout.
	3. This game is suitable for all ages and standards.

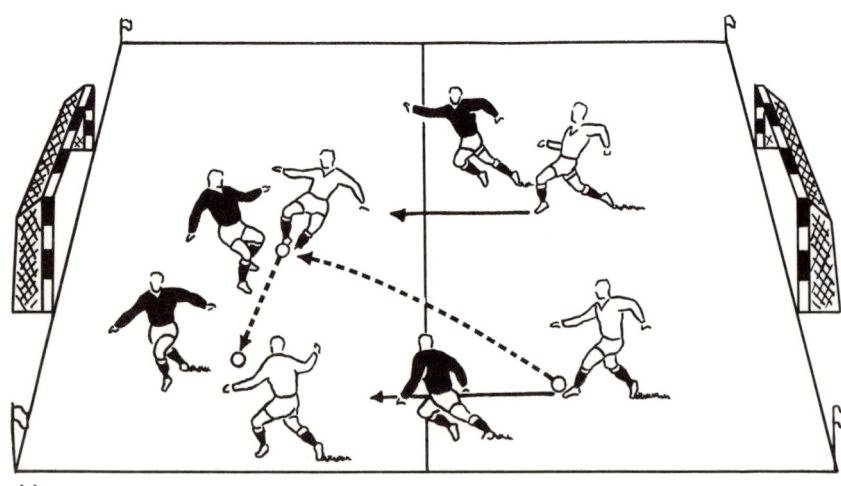

Three Teams, one Goal

Purpose:	Stamina training.
No. of players:	3 teams of 2–3 players and 1 neutral goalkeeper.
Playing area:	One half of the pitch including normal-size goal.
Duration:	40 mins. maximum.
Outline:	One team attacks, trying to score goals. The two other teams defend the goal and try to win the ball. Team in possession always in attack.
Rules:	Play is started by the goalkeeper kicking off. The team gaining possession attacks, and is allowed to shoot from any distance. Play should be interrupted only for fouls, corners and balls out of play. If a goal is scored, the goalkeeper restarts play with another goal-kick.
Possible variation:	To avoid deflected own-goals, a player must have touched the ball before he makes a shot.
Remarks:	Depending on the ability and fitness of players, short intervals should be allowed for practising special techniques.

30   Game with Corner Goals

Purpose:	Stamina training.
No. of players:	2 teams of 5–7 players.
Playing area:	Half the pitch, with a goal at each corner consisting of two touch flags about 2m. apart.
Duration:	60 mins. maximum.
Outline:	Each team has two goals to defend and the two goals of the opposing team to attack. Since the goals are in the corners, the area is more fully utilised, the players having to run further than they have to normally.
Rules:	One team starts the game in its own half. They can attack either of the opponents' two goals, depending on the situation. No goalkeepers. No handling permitted. The play changes direction if the opposition win the ball, if the ball goes out of play, or when a goal is scored.
Possible variations:	1. The last player before the goal may handle the ball. 2. If teams are of 7 or more players the whole pitch should be used.
Remarks:	The smaller the teams, the harder the training.

31   **Full Game with two Balls**

Purpose:	Stamina training.
No. of players:	2 teams of 11 players.
Playing area:	Normal pitch.
Duration:	60 mins. maximum.
Outline:	Each team is given a ball, with which they attack the opposing half and try to score goals. If one team manages to gain possession of the opposition's ball, both balls may be used by them in attack. Since the direction of the play changes often and unexpectedly, the players of both teams have to exert themselves more than usual.
Rules:	The teams kick off in the normal position, i.e. in their own halves. The game is played with proper goalkeepers, but with no offside rule. Corners are taken. When a goal is scored, the goalie restarts play. The normal kick-off is discarded. Two referees are needed for this game, each of whom controls the activity on and around one of the two balls.
Possible variation:	One ball to be played with the right foot, the other only with the left foot.

Game with two open Goals

Purpose:	Stamina training.
No. of players:	2 teams of 2–4 players.
Playing area:	Half normal pitch, with flagposts making two goals each 2m. wide. Distance between goals 20m.
Duration:	30 mins. maximum.
Outline:	One team attacks and tries to score goals, the other defends at the same time trying to win the ball. Since both goals are open, there should be very few interruptions to the game. Both teams are forced to keep running.
Rules:	A goal can be scored from either side of the flagposts. The height of these posts determine the goal, so that balls passing above that height are disallowed. Throw-ins from the touchlines. No proper goalkeepers. Handling is not allowed, nor is it permitted to run between the goalposts. These fouls are penalised by a free kick from 10m. out.
Remarks:	The width of the goal may be altered, 1m. narrower for good players, or extended to 3m. for beginners.
	Fewer players for high ability groups, more players for those with below-average skills.

33   Game with Incomplete Teams

Purpose:	Stamina training.
No. of players:	2 teams of 7–10 players.
Playing area:	Normal soccer pitch.
Duration:	60 mins. maximum.
Outline:	The "missing" players must be compensated for by the players of both sides. In this way the players are forced to exert themselves more than normal.
Rules:	As in a normal game. Only the goalkeeper is nominated, the other positions are filled as the team itself sees fit. Severe demands are made on teamwork; e.g. forwards who are normally only very reluctant defenders can be forced to help the defence if the line-up only provides a team with two defenders.
Possible variations:	To simplify the game, the offside rule can be dispensed with. "One-touch" or "two-touch" passing can be introduced.
Remarks:	Teams of greater ability should include fewer players, those of a lower standard will need more players.

34 Diagonal Game with Four Goals

Purpose:	Stamina training.
No. of players:	2 teams of 6–10 players.
Playing area:	Normal pitch with an additional goal in the middle of each touchline.
Duration:	60 mins. maximum.
Outline:	The attacking team attempts to score in either of their opponents' goals, and likewise to defend their own goals if they lose the ball.
Rules:	A goal is scored when the ball crosses the line of either of the diagonally opposite goals. The attacking team may choose to attack either of the goals. Through good running off the ball and positioning it becomes possible to set up one shooting position after another. There are no proper goalkeepers and no offside rule. The opposition obtains the ball by means of successful tackles, when the ball goes out of play or after fouls.
Possible variation:	The number of passes may be fixed (e.g. unlimited, direct passing).
Remarks:	The fewer the number of players, the more strenuous the game.

35   Six against Six without Goals

Purpose:	Stamina training.
No. of players:	12 players, 6 against 6.
Playing area:	Full pitch.
Duration:	30 mins. maximum in 5-minute periods.
Outline:	The teams try to keep passing the ball among themselves for as long as they can. Initially, first-time passing is required, and this fast tempo is maintained for 5 minutes. After this the pace may be slackened by allowing the ball to be stopped and controlled. One point is given for each successful pass.
Rules:	One team starts the game and continues until they lose the ball to the opposition. Ball possession transfers after successful tackles, balls out of play or if a player does not pass first-time when this is required. In order to count the passes it is absolutely necessary to have one referee per team.
Possible variation:	Begin the game allowing players to play the ball several times, then increase the tempo, allowing the ball to be played only twice by each player, and only then introduce first-time passing. High ability groups should have relatively short breaks, weaker players longer breaks, and play in smaller area.

36   Game with Mobile Goal

Purpose:	Stamina training.
No. of players:	10 players, 5 against 5.
Playing area:	Full pitch.
Duration:	5 × 5 mins., with breaks to change round players.
Outline:	Both teams play at a mobile goal, which consists of two players, one from each team. They carry a pole about 2m. long on their shoulders, and so form the goalposts at either end. This living goal must keep on moving around so that as few goals as possible are scored.
Rules:	One team starts the game in attack. Possession changes after successful tackles or if the ball goes out of play. Play continues directly after each goal with whichever team has the ball. Goals may be scored from either side of the goal. The game is played intensively for 5 minutes. For each period of play two new players substitute as goalposts. Each player must have been goalpost at least once. These are not allowed to stand still, sit or lie down.
Possible variation:	The goal is reduced in size by the carriers hunching or waddling.

37   Game with Goals Back-to-Front

Purpose:	Stamina training.
No. of players:	Two teams of 4–6 players.
Playing area:	Both halves of the pitch. Two goals 20m. apart facing outwards to the sidelines.
Duration:	Maximum 90 mins.
Outline:	One team starts by attacking its opponents' goal, trying to score goals or to avoid conceding goals whenever possession is lost.
Rules:	The game begins with a kick-off from the centre spot. No proper goalkeepers. The last defender of either team is allowed to handle the ball. The play transfers to the other team after a successful tackle, ball in touch, fouls and goals.
Possible variations:	1. The goals may be placed 40m. apart to increase the amount of running that has to be done. 2. The pace can be quickened if play continues immediately after each goal is scored. 3. Handling absolutely forbidden—"Hands" counts as own-goal.
Remarks:	The game can be adapted to suit all ages and standards.

38   Two-Hour Game

Purpose:	Stamina training.
No. of players:	2 teams of 11.
Playing area:	Normal soccer pitch.
Duration:	120 mins. maximum.
Outline:	One team kicks off and attacks the opponents' goal, trying to score. If possession is lost, they defend their own goal.
Rules:	The normal F.A. rules apply, except that in the third period (3 × 40 mins.), the kick-off is decided by tossing again or given to the side who is losing at the time.
Possible variation:	It is possible to divide the game into other periods, e.g. 6 × 20 mins., 4 × 30 mins., 3 × 40 mins., etc.
Remarks:	Since the stamina required is considerable, this game is unsuitable for groups of players less than 18 years of age.

39   Game on a Giant pitch

Purpose:	Stamina training.
No. of players:	2 teams of 11.
Playing area:	250 × 120m. maximum.
Duration:	90 mins. maximum.
Outline:	The teams play normally on this much increased area, attacking their opponents' goal to score, or preventing goals being scored against them when the ball is gained by the other team.
Rules:	Normal F.A. rules to apply.
Possible variations:	1. No offside rule. 2. Balls out of play count as free-kicks. 3. Goals may be increased in size. 4. No proper goalkeepers. The last defender of each team may handle the ball in front of his own goal.
Remarks:	Recreation grounds and airfields as well as ordinary fields are suitable areas for this game.

40 Goal-Kick game

Purpose: Speed training.
No. of players: 6–10 players. Minimum 3 v. 3, maximum 5 v. 5.
Playing area: Both halves, with the centre line marked, the goal areas chalked out, and two hockey goals.
Duration: 40 mins. maximum.
Outline: One team attacks, the other defending its own goal. The attacking team stand on the centre-line and a defender kicks the ball out to them. The attackers then try to make use of their temporary one-man advantage to score before that one defender can sprint up to fill the gap in his team.
Rules: After a goal has been scored or possession lost, the other side retains the ball. Defenders become attackers and take the goal-kick. No handling, no offside.
Possible variation: The sprints can be lengthened or shortened by moving the goals.
Remarks: It's worthwhile nominating players to receive the goal-kick in sequence.

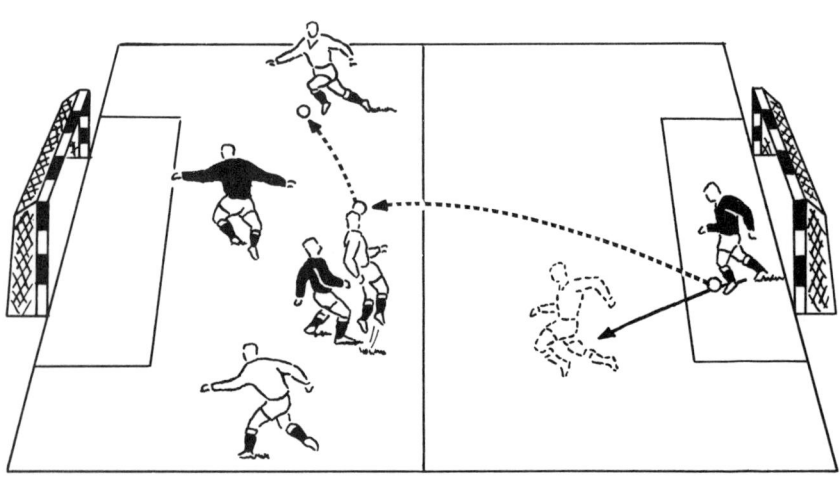

41 Zonal Goals

Purpose:	Training sprinting ability.
No. of players:	2 teams of 3.
Playing area:	70 × 16.5m. (penalty area extended sideways with an 8m. zone marked out at both ends).
Duration:	2 × 10 mins. to 2 × 20 mins.
Outline:	The team attacking tries to pass the ball into their opponents' zone and to bring it under control. If the opposition gains possession, the first team defend their own zone.
Rules:	A point is awarded if the ball is played by one team into the opponents' zone and brought under control by one of that team before it goes out of play. The defence is not allowed into its own zone. Fouls are penalised by indirect free-kicks.
Possible variations:	1. The size of the zones can be varied to suit the skills of the players. The better the players, the smaller the zones. 2. The field may be divided by a centre-line. Points are awarded only when the pass into the zone comes from one or other of the middle areas.
Remarks:	Since the stamina needed for this game is considerable, intervals should be allowed for other exercises.

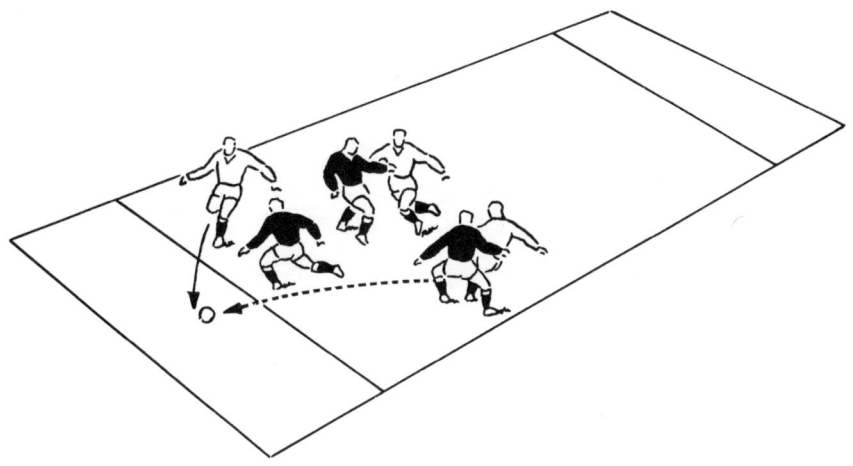

42   Round the Post under Fire

Purpose:	Speed training.
No. of players:	Any number, 3 to a team.
Playing area:	50 × 20m., divided into a "running area" 30m. long and an "in-goal area" of 20 × 20m. A post is put in the ground 20m. in from the touchlines in the "running area".
Duration:	30 mins. maximum.
Outline:	One player stands on the baseline, the two others are in the in-goal area. A point and a free go are awarded to whoever manages to kick the ball out and return to the baseline without his opponents hitting him by throwing the ball at him.
Rules:	Players are numbered 1, 2 and 3. Player No. 1 starts. If his shot into the in-goal area is good, and he succeeds in running round the post back to the line, he is "free", receives one point and can have another try. If, however, he is hit with the ball, he changes places with No. 2, and likewise if his kick lands outside the target area. The two defenders can catch the ball and may cross the "goal-line" carrying the ball so as to be able to throw more accurately at the runner.
Remarks:	Length and breadth of the area, and the distance to the post, to be suited to the capabilities of the players.

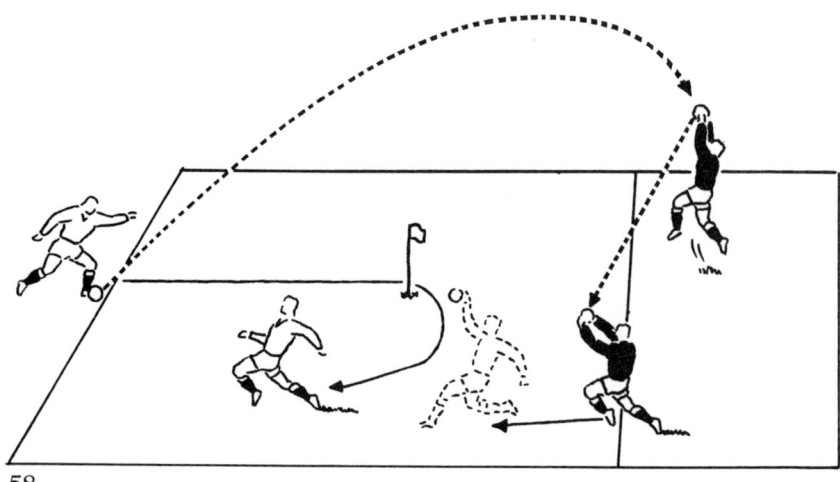

43   Sprinting on to Goal-Kick

Purpose:	Speed training.
No. of players:	3.
Playing area:	Half normal pitch (where goal-line crosses sides of penalty box to be well marked as start).
Duration:	30 mins. or 20 sprints.
Outline:	All players try to be first to the ball, wrong-foot the other man and score a goal.
Rules:	One player is goalkeeper, the other two stand at either side of him on their marks. The goalkeeper kicks into the middle. As he kicks, the other two men sprint to the ball. The first one there is awarded one point. He can gain another point by dribbling round the other man and shooting. After each shot the game restarts as before.
Possible variations:	1. Start sprints from various places. 2. If the two players sprinting are of unequal speed, the goal-kick should be placed correspondingly.
Remarks:	Training for speed-stamina is also possible if the pauses are shortened.

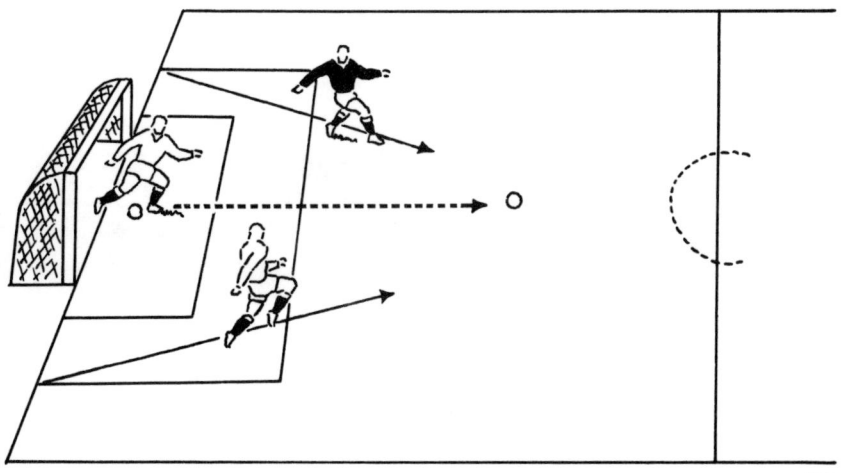

44 Pair-Sprinting with Ball

Purpose:	Speed training.
No. of players:	2 groups of 4 plus 2 goalkeepers.
Playing area:	Normal pitch, including a well marked centre-circle.
Duration:	30 mins. maximum or 5 sprints for each player.
Outline:	Each of four players is teamed up with an opponent, each pair having a ball. When a name is called, that player sprints toward a goal, dribbling the ball and aiming to score. His "shadow" sprints after him in order to defend the goal.
Rules:	The player may attack either goal. If his opponent manages to rob him of the ball, the game is stopped and that pair return to the centre-circle, which may be left only when the appropriate name is called. If a foul is committed, the defender is awarded the ball, plus a start of 3m.
Possible variations:	1. If the defender gains the ball with a fair tackle he may be allowed to attempt to score himself. 2. The pair may begin the game in turns without names being called.
Remarks:	All players must perform the same number of sprints: the best way is with a checklist.

45   Sprinting to Ball in Centre

Purpose:	Speed training.
No. of players:	2 teams of 4.
Playing area:	40 × 20m., centre-line marked out; two hockey goals.
Duration:	30 mins. maximum or up to 20 sprints.
Outline:	Sprinting to a ball and scoring past a defender, the goals scored by one team to be totalled up.
Rules:	The four players of either team line up at each end. On the word "go" from the coach they sprint to the balls in the centre. Whoever gets to the ball first dribbles it towards the goal at the far end and shoots. If he scores, he may then go to the aid of any other player of his own team.
Possible variations:	1. Vary the size of playing area and/or number of players. 2. Only defence or only attack to be allowed to assist their team-mates.
Remarks:	If the size of pitch or number of players is changed, ensure that the players do not obstruct each other.

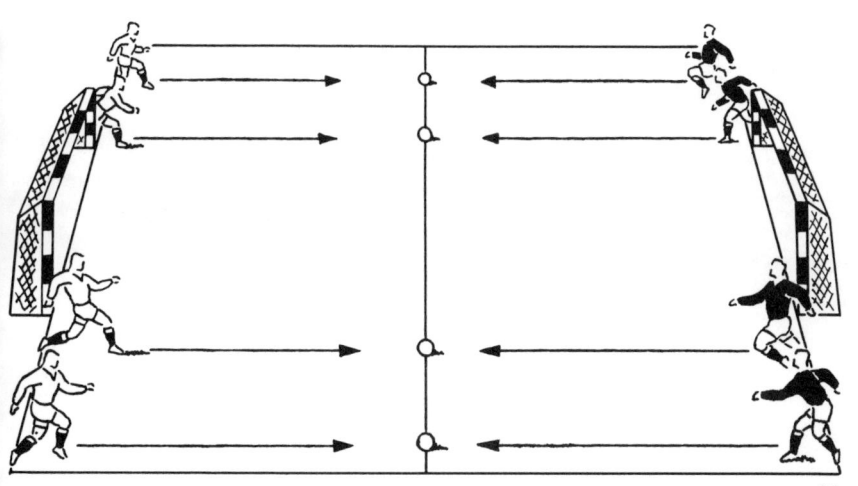

46 Chinese Soccer-Tennis

Purpose:	Speed training.
No. of players:	4; 2 v. 2.
Playing area:	16 × 16m., with a net 1m. high across the centre.
Duration:	Best of three games of 21 points.
Outline:	The ball must be kicked across the net into the opponents' court. After the ball has been played, the player changes ends. The opposite side is awarded a point when a fault occurs.
Rules:	The game is started by the ball being served from the base-line. The ball must bounce once in the opposite half, and may be played only once. Service changes with each fault. A fault occurs when the ball is touched by a player who has not changed ends; when it is not allowed to bounce or allowed to bounce more than once; when the service hits the net or lands outside the court; when the ball is handled or played more than once consecutively.
Possible variations:	1. Players without the requisite skills may let the ball bounce more than once. 2. Changing ends can be made more difficult by placing obstacles at the sides of the net.

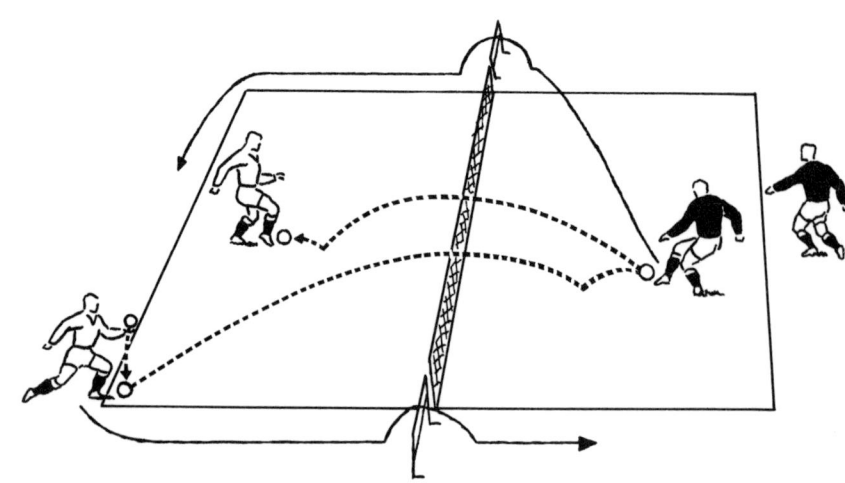

47 Round the Flagpost in Teams

Purpose:	Speed training.
No. of players:	2 teams of 4–10 players.
Playing area:	Both halves of a pitch, with a flagpost placed on the centre spot.
Duration:	20 sprints maximum.
Outline:	The two teams line up at either end of the area. One team kicks off into the opponents' half and immediately sprints off round the flagpost and back. The other team catches the ball and by quick interpassing hit as many of the opposition as possible by throwing the ball.
Rules:	Each member of the other team hit counts one point. One point also if the original kick-off does not reach the other half or if any of the team do not run round the flagpost. After each run, the rôles of the two teams are reversed. The winning team is decided only when every player has kicked off.
Possible variation:	The receiving team are not allowed to pass, but must shy directly.
Remarks:	Adapt the size of pitch and number of repetitions to the standard of the players.

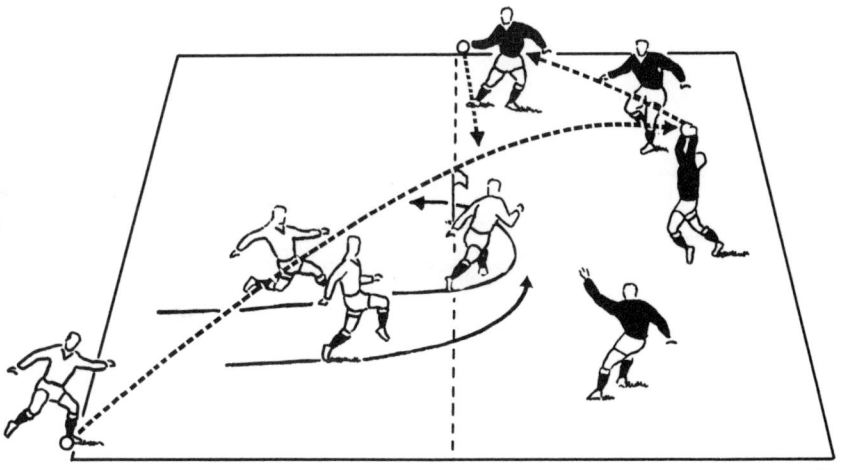

48 Running Backwards Game

Purpose:	Training for running backwards.
No. of players:	12; 6 v. 6.
Playing area:	Full pitch.
Duration:	20 mins. maximum.
Outline:	The three forwards of each team are forced to run backwards. They may pass back only to the defence, who are running forward to score their team's goals.
Rules:	The forwards may stop running backwards if their team loses the ball, but must recommence if possession is regained by their defence, when the ball goes out of play, or when the other team scores. These three forwards may not leave the opposing half. No proper goalkeepers. No handling the ball. The three forwards change places with the backs every five minutes. Goals scored by the forwards back-heeling also count.
Possible variation:	For schools or youth-clubs, running or hopping sideways can be substituted for running backwards. Ensure that the strenuousness of this game and the change-over between forwards and backs suits the capabilities of the players.

49   Soccer-Tennis with Touch-Post

Purpose: Speed training.

No. of players: 6; 3 v. 3.

Playing area: 20 × 40m., with a net across the centre (a string or some hurdles would also be sufficient). 3m. behind the baselines a flagpost (or medicine ball, box-lid etc.).

Duration: Best of three games of 21 points. If both teams each win a game they change ends after 10 points of the decider.

Outline: The ball is served by being kicked into the opponents' court. The player who last plays the ball can take part in the game again only after having touched the post. A minus point for each mistake made.

Rules: The ball is served from behind the baseline. The type of service allowed should be dependent on the ability of the players. The ball may be served as a spotkick, drop-kick or ordinary punt. The ball must bounce once in the opposite court before being returned. Service changes after every fault. A fault occurs when the ball:
1. is returned by a player who was also the previous player, i.e. who has not touched the post.
2. is allowed to bounce twice, or is returned before it has bounced at all.
3. touches the net on service, or bounces outside the boundary lines.
4. is handled, or played more than once or if a player infringes the opposition court.

Possible variations:
1. Post or other marker to be touched with the left or right-hand, either foot, or sat on.
2. If, as with particularly good players, the game moves so fast that they can return only with great difficulty to meet the ball after having touched the post, the law should state that every player on each side should play the ball before it can be returned.
3. It can be decided to kick with either the left or right foot only.

Remarks: The distance from the field of play to the post can be varied according to the standard of the players. It would also be possible to put other posts on either corner, so that the player has the option which he touches, whereby the disruption of running back and forth is reduced to a minimum.

50   Round the Post and Back

Purpose:	Speed training.
No. of players:	Any number, but teams to be of equal strength.
Playing area:	Baseline, with two posts or medicine balls placed 20–30m. away.
Duration:	20 mins. maximum, or ten sprints for each team.
Outline:	The players of each team attempt to run as fast as possible round a flagpost and back to the baseline while dribbling the ball. The team finishing first is the winner, and a point is awarded for each win.
Rules:	On the word go, the first men in each team sprint off, round the flagpost and back, passing the ball to the next man on the line. He then sprints off. A flying start means disqualification. The exercise is finished when the last man of the first team is back over the start-line.
Possible variations:	1. Shorten or lengthen the distance to be run. 2. Ball to be passed to the next man as soon as player has rounded the post.
Remarks:	Suit the distance to be covered to the fitness of the players.

51   Hurdle Relay

Purpose: Speed training.
No. of players: Any number, but teams to be of equal strength.
Playing area: 2 lines of hurdles about 30 or 40m. long.
Duration: 20 mins. maximum or ten sprints per man.
Outline: Players of both teams attempt to play the ball through the hurdle and leap over after it; after having cleared the final one they dribble the ball back alongside the hurdles to the starting line. One point is awarded to the team winning each relay.
Rules: The front men of each team start off on the word go. The next man goes only when he receives the ball from his team-mate behind the starting line. Flying starts mean disqualification. A relay is finished when the last man of a team has recrossed the starting line.
Possible variations:
1. The ball may be played over or around the hurdles.
2. Players to run round or crawl through the hurdles.
Remarks: Suit the length of run and height of hurdles to the abilities of the players.

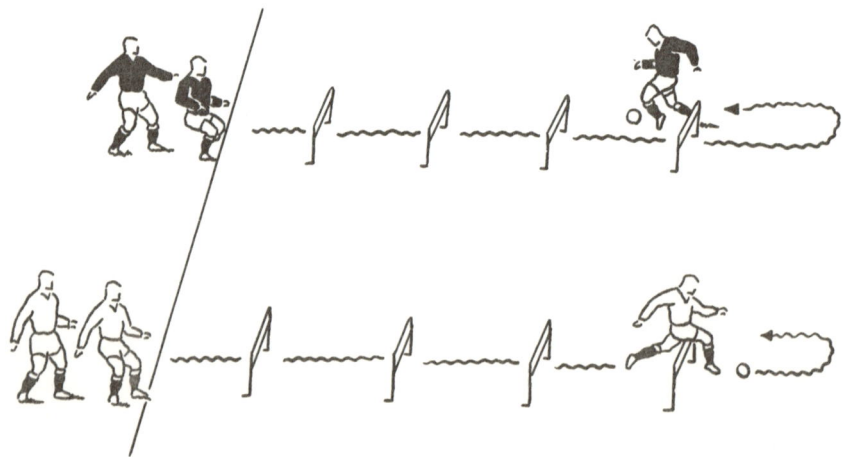

52 Soccer on Horseback

Purpose:	Development of leg muscles.
No. of players:	12; 3 against 3, each carrying one man on his back.
Playing area:	Approximately 15 × 16.50m.
Duration:	1 min. action, 1 min. pause.
Outline:	To score, teams must make the ball cross the opponents' goal-line.
Rules:	One team starts the game by attacking their opponents' goal. Dribbling the ball across the goal-line counts as a goal, and the ball then goes to the opposing side. The men being carried may not interfere in the game by obstructing other players. Pairs change over every minute.
Possible variations:	1. Action phases may be increased to 2 mins. 2. Obstruction may be allowed.
Remarks:	Suit the size of playing area to the abilities of the players. This exercise is not advisable for younger players, since the weight of the rider can cause physical damage.

53 Crab Soccer

Purpose:	Skill and agility training.
No. of players:	2 teams of 4–6 players.
Playing area:	20 × 10m. Two hockey-sized goals placed on the sidelines.
Duration:	20 mins. maximum.
Outline:	One team attacks and attempts to score goals, and if the ball-possession is lost, to avoid conceding goals.
Rules:	With the exception of the goalies, all players may move only crab-fashion, and may play the ball only in this position. Handling is forbidden, except for the goalies. The hands must always be in contact with the ground. A free-kick is given if these rules are infringed. Goalkeepers may catch the ball with their hands, and are permitted to kneel. They should fetch all the balls that go out of play in their half. The game is restarted by an indirect free-kick. No offside rule.
Possible variation:	Effort can be increased if players are not allowed to sit at all.
Remarks:	The number of players may be increased to 8 and the playing area to 30 × 15m. This game is particularly suited for the gymnasium.

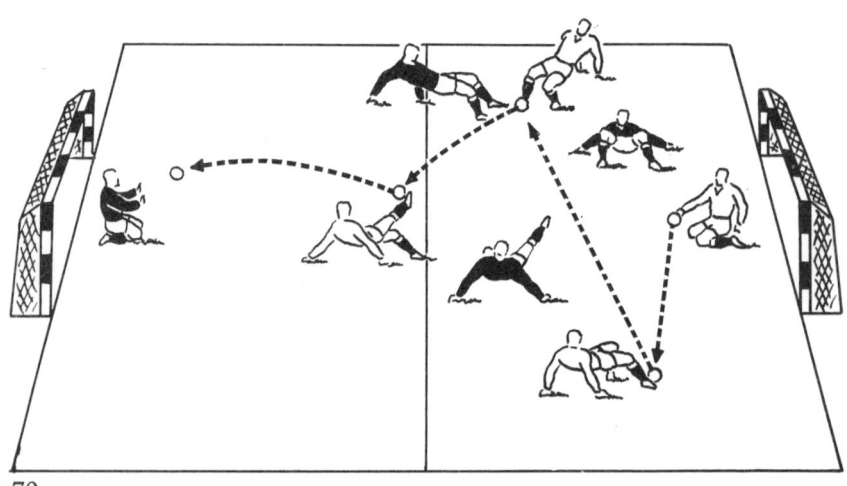

Skill-training games

54   No Bodily Contact

Purpose:	Training of ball-skills.
No. of players:	8. 4 v. 4.
Playing area:	40 × 25m. Two hockey goals.
Duration:	40 mins. maximum.
Outline:	Each team attacks the opponents' half, trying to score goals. The defending team may not defend in the normal manner. Only the path of attacker or ball may be blocked.
Rules:	The game is started by one player passing the ball to another. The ball must not touch the ground, nor may it be played more than three times consecutively by any one player. The opposition is awarded the ball if it touches the ground, or if it's played four or more times consecutively. No proper goalkeepers. Handling not allowed.
Remarks:	For less skilled players, the three-times-only rule may be abandoned. For technically proficient players twice should be the maximum. This exercise is particularly suited for those players already adept at football skills.

55 Game with three 'Neutrals'

Purpose:	Training of ball-skills.
No. of players:	2 teams of 4, plus 3 "neutral" players.
Playing area:	40 × 25m., two hockey goals.
Duration:	40 mins. maximum.
Outline:	Each team attempts to attack its opponents' half, to score goals. The neutral players are always on the side of the attackers to give them numerical superiority.
Rules:	The game starts with one player passing the ball to a team-mate. The ball must not touch the ground, nor may it be played more than three times consecutively by any one player. The opposition is awarded the ball after a successful interception, if the ball is played four or more times by one player or if it touches the ground. No proper goalkeepers. Handling not permitted.
Possible variation:	The number of times a player may play the ball can be varied from unlimited down to once only.
Remarks:	The smaller the teams and the greater the number of neutrals, the easier the game becomes (e.g. 2 v. 2 plus 5).

56 'Piggy' with Ball in the Air

Purpose:	Practising ball-skills.
No. of players:	4–5. 3 or 4 against one.
Playing area:	10 × 10m.
Duration:	20 mins. maximum.
Outline:	Three or four players spread out over the area and give high passes to each other. "Piggy" tries to touch the ball, and thus change places with the player who kicked it.
Rules:	Without allowing the ball to touch the ground, a player may juggle it as much as he wishes and choose his time to make the pass. Apart from when he intercepts the ball, "Piggy" also leaves the middle if one of the passers allows the ball to touch the ground or it goes out of play. Hands not allowed.
Possible variations:	1. Ball to be played a maximum of twice consecutively. 2. First-time passing only.
Remarks:	This game is suitable for all players who have mastered the basics of soccer technique.

57 Soccer Tennis (Singles)

Purpose:	Training for taking and giving passes.
No. of players:	2. 1 against 1.
Playing area:	12 × 16m. Divided across the middle by a net 1m. high.
Duration:	Best of three sets of 21 points.
Outline:	A point is given when a player plays the ball over the net into his opponent's half. The ball may be played only once. The set is won by the first player to 21, the winner being the first one to win two sets. In a third set decider, players change ends after 10 points.
Rules:	One player serves from behind his base-line by kicking the ball over the net. It may bounce once in the other court before being returned. The ball may be volleyed with the head or foot. Each player has five consecutive serves, taken after a fault. A fault occurs when the ball is served directly into the net, lands outside the court, bounces more than once or is handled.
Possible variation:	Various types of kicks to be used for service.
Remarks:	Suit the size of the area to the players' ability.

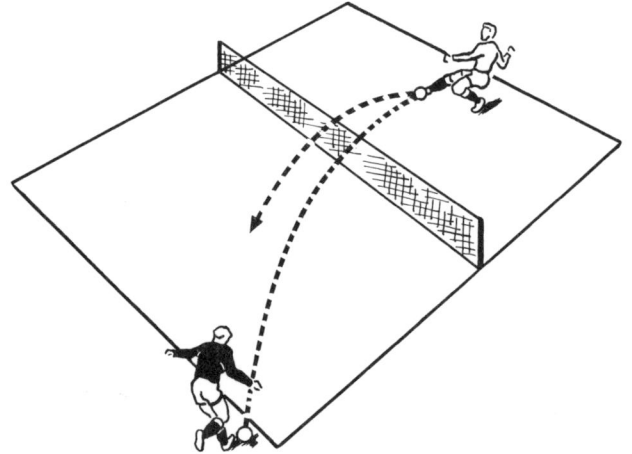

58   Soccer Tennis (Doubles)

Purpose:	Training for receiving and giving passes.
No. of players:	4. 2 *v.* 2.
Playing area:	16 × 8m., divided across the middle by a net 1m. high and lengthwise into two halves.
Duration:	Best of three sets of 21 points.
Outline:	A point is given when a player plays the ball over the net into his opponents' half. The ball may be played only once. The set is won by the first player to 21. The winner is the first one to win two sets. In a third set decider, players change ends after 10 points.
Rules:	One player serves from behind his base-line by kicking the ball over the net. It may bounce once in the other court before being returned. The ball may be volleyed with the head or foot. Each player has five consecutive serves, taken after a fault, i.e. when the ball is served directly into the net, lands outside the court, bounces more than once or is handled. The following rules also apply:

1. The service is given from the right-hand court into the left-hand opposite court. Only then may the ball be played into either of the opposite courts.

2. The ball is always played alternately. The player who has just played the ball must leave the return to his partner. Consecutive play by one player counts as a fault, and as a point for the opposition.

	3. Players change courts after each change of service.
Possible variation:	Various types of kicks to be used for service.
Remarks:	This game is suitable for all ages and standards.

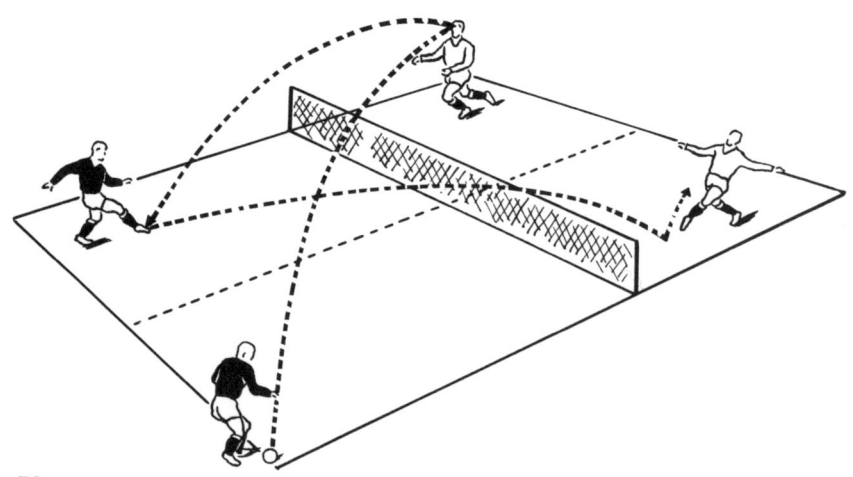

59 Soccer Tennis (Teams)

Purpose:	Training for taking and giving passes.
No. of players:	2 teams of 3 or 4.
Playing area:	About 10 × 20m., divided by a net 1m. high into two courts.
Duration:	As No. 57.
Outline:	As No. 57.
Rules:	As No. 57, but following rules also apply:

1. Players of both teams are numbered 1 to 3 or 1 to 4. This is important since the ball must be served by a different player each time. The team moves round clockwise so that each player arrives at the service corner.
2. The ball may be played three or even four times if agreed among one team. It is permissible that one player plays the ball twice if another team member touches it inbetween. One player touching the ball more than once consecutively is not allowed in this variation either.

Possible variation:	As No. 57.
Remarks:	Suitable for all ages and levels.

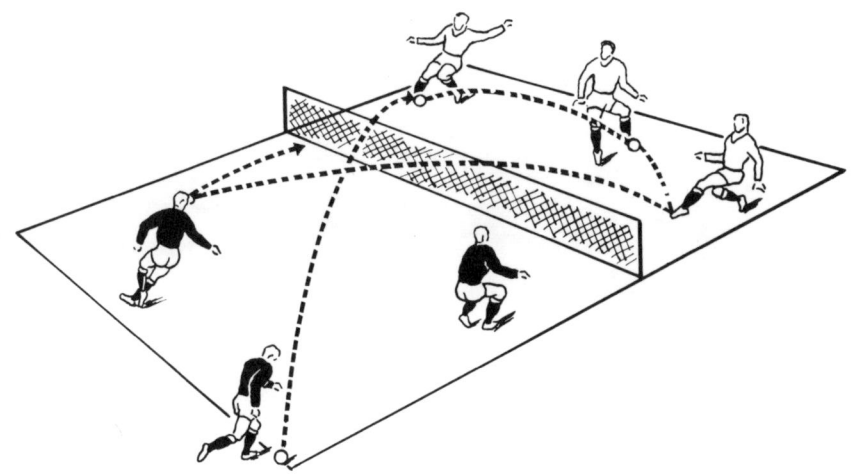

60   Soccer Tennis with Dead Zone

Purpose: Training for taking and giving passes.
No. of players: 2 teams of 2.
Playing area: 22 × 8m., divided into halves by a net 1m. high. Two parallel lines are drawn 3m. from either side of the net, marking dead zone.
Duration: As No. 57.
Outline: As No. 57.
Rules: As No. 57 with following special rules:
1. To win a point the ball must clear both the net and the dead zone. Since the ball must therefore be kicked a greater distance, greater demands are made on the skill of the players. If the ball bounces in the dead zone it counts as a fault, and as a point for the opposition.
2. Playing the ball several times consecutively is permitted in this game, as are any number of passes among one team. It is, however, important that the ball should bounce only once here, too.
Possible variation: As No. 57.
Remarks: Depth of the dead zone should be suited to the ability of the players.

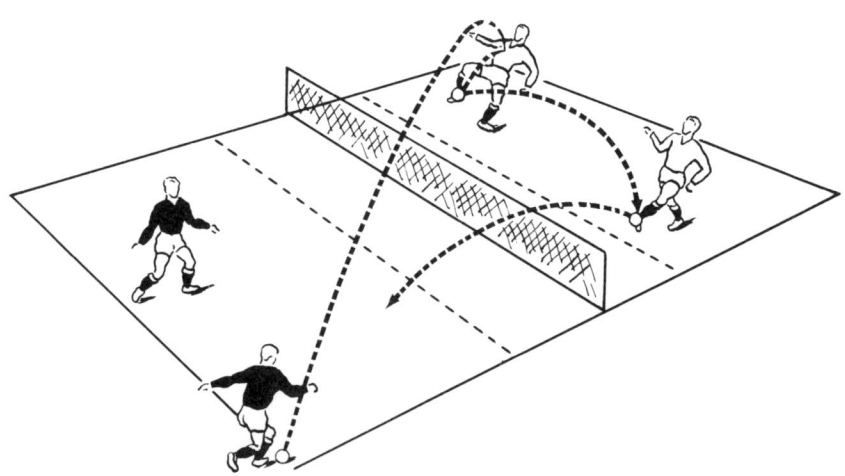

61 Soccer Tennis between two Ropes

Purpose:	Training for passing accurately.
No. of players:	2 teams of 3.
Playing area:	18 × 9m., divided into halves by two parallel ropes, (1m. and 3m. above the ground).
Duration:	As No. 57.
Outline:	As No. 57.
Rules:	Each team alternately has five services. The ball is served from behind each team's base-line after a fault, which occurs when the ball:
	1. does not pass between the ropes.
	2. lands outside the area.
	3. bounces more than once.
	4. is handled.
	Play may continue if the ball touches the ropes, as long as it finally passes between them.
Possible variation:	As No. 57.
Remarks:	The distance between the ropes may be made progressively narrower to suit the ability of the teams.

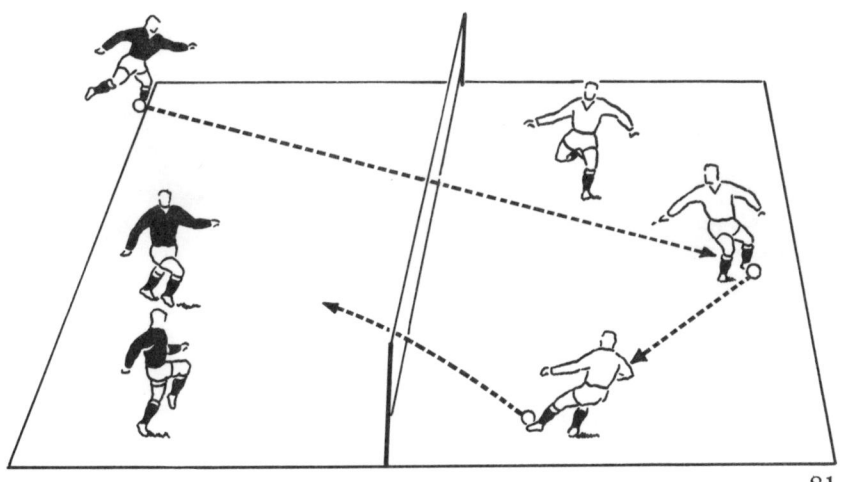

62 Four-Ball Battle

Purpose: Free-kick training.
No. of players: 2 teams of 5–10.
Playing area: Extended penalty area, with a centre line 2m. wide.
Duration: 15 mins. maximum.
Outline: Teams attempt to kick all the balls into their opponents' area. If they succeed, a minus point is counted against the opponents. The winner is the team with the least penalty-points.
Rules: Each team has four balls. On the whistle, the teams kick all the balls into their opponents' half. If all the balls are simultaneously in one half the game is stopped and a point deducted from that team in whose half the balls lie. The balls are then lined up again, and the exercise re-starts. The 2m.-wide central area must not be entered. First-time shooting only.
Possible variations: 1. Any player who does not "score" drops out until a point is scored by either side.
2. The method used for the free-kick may be fixed.
Remarks: Particularly suitable for the gym.

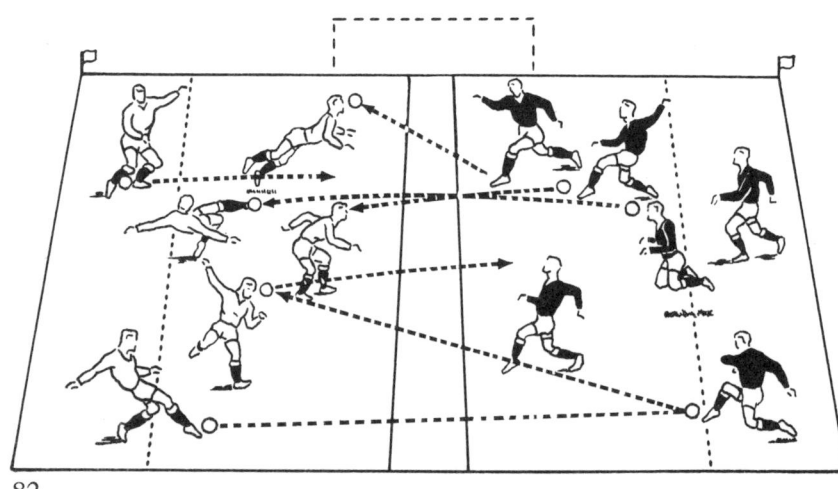

63 Rebound Soccer Tennis

Purpose:	Training of ball-skills.
No. of players:	2 teams of 2.
Playing area:	One front wall with a line 1 × 2m. high. A line on the ground 4m. from the wall, and a 10m.-wide playing area.
Duration:	Best of three 15-point games.
Outline:	One team kicks the ball from the 4m.-line against the wall. It must bounce back over the line and bounce once in the playing area before being returned by the other team. Faults count one point for the opposition.
Rules:	The game is started with a kick-off from the 4m.-line. Service changes after each fault. A fault occurs when the ball:
	1. bounces between the wall and the 4m.-line.
	2. hits the wall below the line.
	3. bounces more than once.
	4. is played more than once by the same player.
Possible variation:	Method used for serve may be fixed.
Remarks:	The dimensions of the court must be adapted for the players concerned. Beginners to play without a 4m.-line.

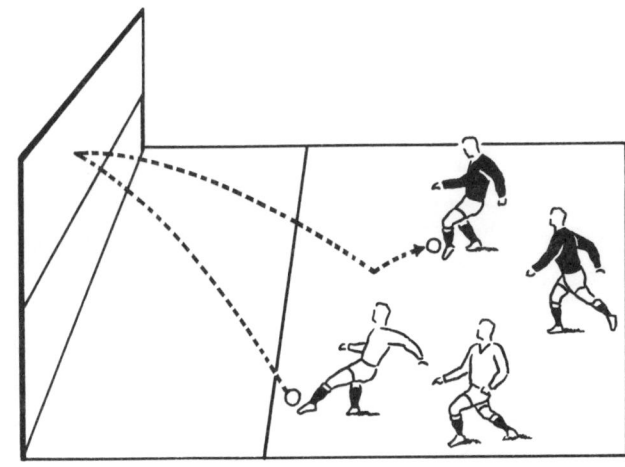

64   Game with Many Goals

Purpose:	Training for pass with the inside of the foot.
No. of players:	2 teams of 5.
Playing area:	Half pitch, six auxiliary goals (flagposts) 1m. wide.
Duration:	60 mins. maximum.
Outline:	Both teams attempt to kick the ball with inside of foot through one of the goals and score, or, if the other team is in possession, to avoid conceding goals.
Rules:	A goal is scored when the ball crosses the goal-line between the flagposts and reaches a member of the same team. A shot passing above the posts does not count. Goals may be scored from either side of the goals. The game carries on without pause after a score. Consecutive scores through the same goal are not allowed.
Possible variation:	Goals may be scored only with either the right or left foot.
Remarks:	The number and the width of the goals should be suited to the capabilities of the players. Teams of six or over should use a full-size pitch. This game should not be played between teams of unequal numbers.

65   Double-Zone Game

Purpose:	Training for long, side-footed cross.
No. of players:	2 teams of 8.
Playing area:	Full pitch with well-marked centre-line.
Duration:	40 mins. maximum.
Outline:	In each of the halves, four defenders play four attackers. The attackers attempt to score goals, while the defence tries to stop any score.
Rules:	If the defenders manage to win the ball, they pass it to their attack in the other half. No player may cross the centre-line. The midfield is crossed by long passing. No offside.
Possible variations:	1. Instead of a centre-line, a 20m.-wide central zone can be marked which may not be entered by any player. 2. The defenders must manage to move the ball out of their half with a maximum of three passes. 3. Number of players may be increased to twelve a side.
Remarks:	It's possible to favour either defence or attack by altering the incentives.

Game with 5m.-Zone Goals

Purpose:	Training for pass with inside of foot.
No. of players:	2 teams of 6.
Playing area:	40 × 10m., with two 5m.-wide zones at either side.
Duration:	30 mins. maximum.
Outline:	The teams are divided into three defenders in the 5m.-zone, and three attackers in midfield. The attackers try to score by shooting through the players in the 5m.-zone, who in turn are attempting to prevent goals.
Rules:	A goal is scored when the ball crosses the rear line of the 5m.-zone. Players may use only the inside of the foot. The 5m.-zone line may not be crossed in either direction. The attack and defence change round every five minutes. Handling is not permitted to prevent a goal, nor are passes above head height. Any infringements are penalised by an indirect free-kick.
Possible variations:	1. Limit number of times ball may be played. 2. Fix which foot to be used.
Remarks:	Suitable for all ages and standards.

67 Passing the Middle Man

Purpose:	Training for pass with inside of foot.
No. of players:	3.
Playing area:	24 × 8m. divided into three equal squares of 8 × 8m.
Duration:	30 mins. maximum.
Outline:	The two outside men try to pass to each other past the middle man, not allowing him to touch it. The man in the middle tries to intercept the ball. The winner is the player with the least penalty-points.
Rules:	One player in each zone. The two outside players pass to each other on the half-volley. The man in the middle tries to intercept, using legitimate soccer methods. Passes may bounce only once. A penalty point is awarded against a player if he lets the ball bounce more than once, if his pass bounces outside the target area, or if the middle man intercepts. Positions should be changed at regular intervals.
Possible variations:	1. Fix which foot to be used. 2. If necessary allow ball to be played twice.

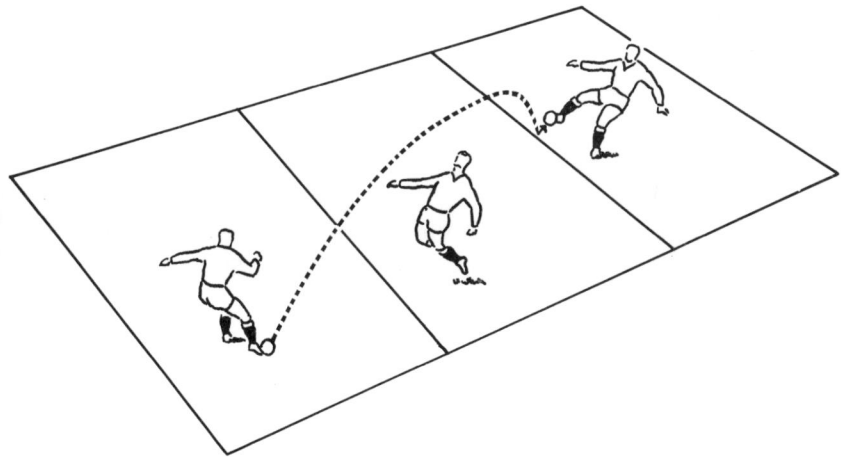

68   Shooting at Individual Goals

Purpose: Training for pass with inside of foot.
No. of players: 2 teams. Any number of players.
Playing area: Chalk out several areas of 20 × 6m. and place two flagposts 50m. apart in the middle of each one.
Duration: 30 mins. maximum.
Outline: Every player tries to shoot through his goal and score. The winner is the man with the highest score after a given time.
Rules: A goal is scored when the ball is kicked from behind the base-line through the posts. If the shot goes over the posts, the ball goes to the opponent, no goal being scored. Goals scored by directly volleyed shots count double. Change sides after half the time has elapsed. Each team should count its own goals.
Possible variations: 1. Fix which foot to be used.
2. Lengthen the areas up to a maximum of 40m.
Remarks: A goal-net may be set up on the base-lines to minimise the effect of in- and out-swingers. Game suitable for playground or other hard surface.

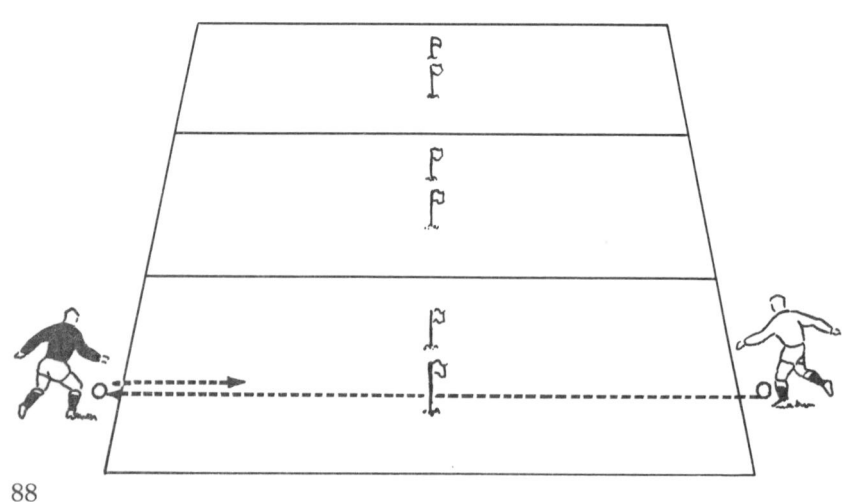

69 Single Circular Target

Purpose:	Training for pass with inside of foot.
No. of players:	2 teams of 3.
Playing area:	Half a normal pitch containing a circle of 8m. diameter with a medicine ball in the middle as target.
Duration:	30 mins. maximum.
Outline:	The team in possession attacks and tries to hit the medicine ball; when possession is lost they defend the circle.
Rules:	Teams compete for points. The circle may not be entered. If the ball goes out of play or stops within the circle, a throw-in continues the game. After each hit the medicine ball must be replaced on its spot.
Possible variation:	The number of players may be altered: if an odd number, the extra man plays with the attackers so that they have numerical superiority.
Remarks:	This game is also suitable for small gymnasia, where the wall-bars can be used as "cushions", as in billiards.

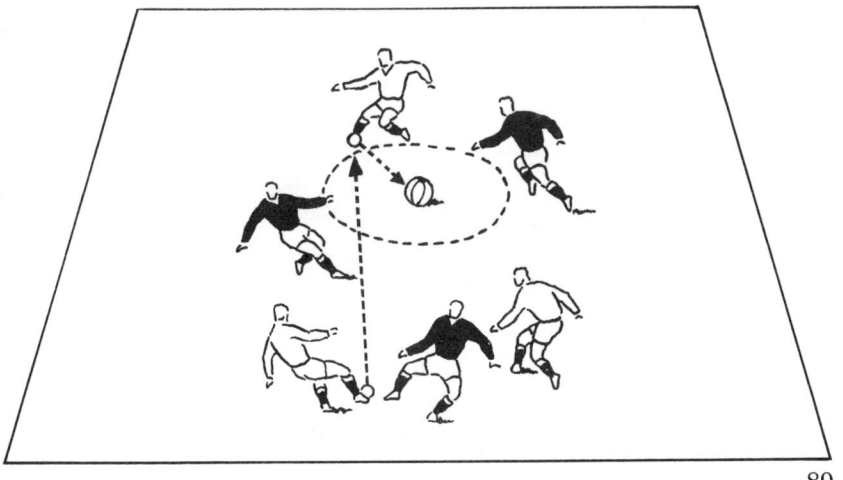

70 Double Circular Target

Purpose:	Training to pass with inside of foot.
No. of players:	2 teams of 4.
Playing area:	Half the pitch: two circles of 8m. diameter each, equal distance from the centre and with a medicine ball in the middle.
Duration:	50 mins. maximum.
Outline:	Each team has its own circle. One team tries to score off the ball in the middle of the opponents' circle, the other team trying to intercept. Each hit scores a point.
Rules:	The ball goes to the opposition after each score or if the opposition pick up the loose ball. No player may enter either circle. A free-kick is given at the place of any infringement. The medicine ball is replaced on its spot only if it rolls outside the circle.
Possible variations:	1. Increase the diameter of the circles to 15m. 2. Fix which foot to be used.
Remarks:	Teams of relatively little ability can play with an extra man on the attacking side.

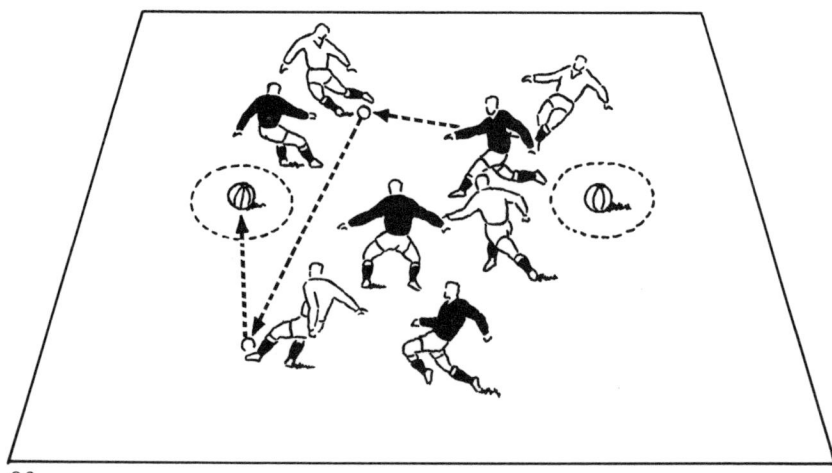

71 Soccer Skittles

Purpose:	Training for pass with inside of foot.
No. of players:	2 teams of 3–4.
Playing area:	40 × 20m. with an area 3m. wide along each side, three skittles placed at an equal distance inside both these areas.
Duration:	30 mins. maximum.
Outline:	A team defends its own skittles and attempts to knock over its opponents' skittles with the ball. A goal for each skittle hit.
Rules:	Teams line up in their own halves. One team attacks the other's skittles, attempting to put down as many as possible. If the ball is lost, the side now in possession attacks. Likewise with balls out of play, or successful shots. The skittle area may not be entered. Skittles which are hit remain down, to show the score.
Possible variation:	It should be decided at the outset whether shots are allowed off either foot, or whether only with the left or right.
Remarks:	This game is particularly suitable for the gymnasium. In this case, however, shots rebounding from the wallbars and hitting a skittle do not count.

72 Game with Four Parallel Zones

Purpose:	Training for pass with inside of foot.
No. of players:	16, 8 v. 8.
Playing area:	40 × 20m., the area divided laterally into four equal zones.
Duration:	20 mins. maximum.
Outline:	Both teams are divided into groups of four, each group lining up in alternate zones to the opposition. Points are gained if the ball can be passed through the opposition to the other half of the team.
Rules:	One team starts by interpassing until a gap is created through which the ball can be passed. Ball-possession changes if the pass is intercepted, or if the pass sends ball out of play. Handling not allowed. Players must remain in their own zones. Passes may not be above head height.
Possible variations:	1. Limit number of passes allowed within one group. 2. Fix which foot to be used and for number of times ball may be played. 3. Use two balls.
Remarks:	If two balls are used, two referees will be required to follow each ball.

73 Passing to Outnumbered Man

Purpose:	Training for pass with inside of foot.
No. of players:	2 teams of 4–6.
Playing area:	Penalty area with 3m.-wide zone down the middle.
Duration:	20 mins. maximum.
Outline:	Each team has its own half, with one player positioned in the opposing half. He must move around cleverly enough to enable his team-mates to find him with a pass. Each successfully taken pass allows another player to come into the opposition half. The game is won by the team which has all its players in one half.
Rules:	The central zone may not be entered. Interpassing is allowed to create the right opportunity to pass. Ball-possession changes if a pass is intercepted or if the ball goes out of play.
Possible variations:	1. Limit interpassing to three passes. 2. Fix which foot to be used. 3. Outside of foot may also be used.
Remarks:	For less skilful groups, the playing area can be extended to make it easier to pass correctly.

74 Six-Goal Game

Purpose:	Training for pass with inside of foot.
No. of players:	2 teams of 12.
Playing area:	Across one half, with six goals of equal width down either side.
Duration:	60 mins. maximum.
Outline:	Each team is divided into two groups. Six players keep their six goals, the other six play against the other team, attacking the oppositions' goals or trying to win the ball.
Rules:	After each goal scored, the goalies change positions with the others (alternative: every 5 minutes). Each goalie has only one goal and may handle only in front of that goal. Passes and shots are limited to head height. Goals are scored only if the ball passes below the top of the flagposts. Shots may be only side-footed. Infringements are penalised by a free-kick. No offside rule. Balls out of play are thrown in.
Possible variations:	1. Fix which foot to be used for shooting; allow other than side-footed shots. 2. Goalies may assist each other.
Remarks:	Particularly suitable for school classes and younger groups.

75 Random Flagposts

Purpose:	Training for pass with inside of foot.
No. of players:	2, 4 or 8.
Playing area:	Centre circle with flagposts stuck in at random.
Duration:	2 mins. maximum.
Outline:	Two players dribble a ball round the perimeter of the circle and try to pass the ball through the flagposts to win points.
Rules:	Passes must be made from outside the circle. The player who passes must run on to intercept the ball in a new position. Passes must pass inside at least two flagposts.
Possible variations:	1. The number of flagposts can be increased or reduced. 2. The diameter of the circle may be altered. 3. The position of the flagposts can be (constantly) changed.
Remarks:	Suitable for all ages and standards.

76 Two Against Two Round Centre Circle

Purpose:	Training for pass with inside of foot.
No. of players:	2 teams of 2.
Playing area:	Centre circle including centre line.
Duration:	20 mins. maximum.
Outline:	One player of each team stands on the edge of the circle in one half and has to pass the ball across to his team-mate to gain one point.
Rules:	The game begins with a bounce-up. The winner of the ball gains one point if he manages to pass successfully to his team-mate across the circle. The players may not enter the circle, nor may passes be made which do not pass through the circle. No intervals. The pass must be made at the latest after three attempts. The important thing is the running done by the player waiting for the pass. Signals are allowed.
Remarks:	To start with, the passes may be taken inside the circle as long as they cross the centre line. Later the full width should be used. This game is better suited to more skilful players.

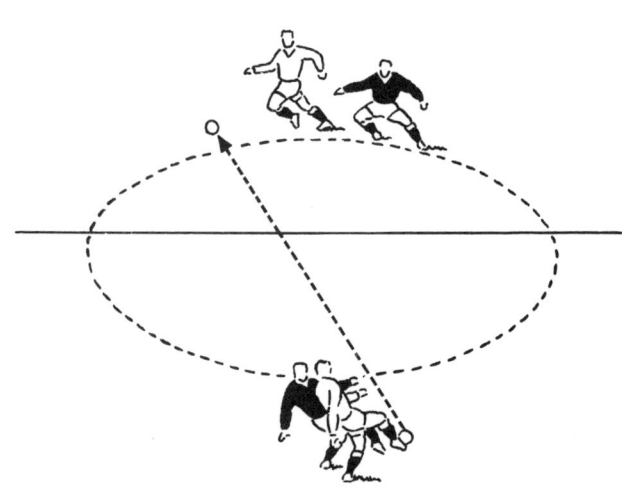

77 Tiger-Ball

Purpose:	Training for pass with inside of foot.
No. of players:	6–8.
Playing area:	Circle of about 6m. diameter.
Duration:	20 mins. maximum.
Outline:	One player stands inside the circle. The others form a circle round the edge and pass the ball to each other. The one in the circle tries to intercept the passes.
Rules:	The ball may be passed in any direction. First-time passing only. If the man in the circle manages to touch the ball he changes places with the player who last passed it. Likewise if the ball is passed other than side-footed, or if it goes above head height.
Possible variations:	1. The ball to be passed only with the left or the right foot. 2. With more than eight players, two men stand inside the circle.
Remarks:	For less skilful players it will be necessary either to extend the circle or allow players to play the ball twice.

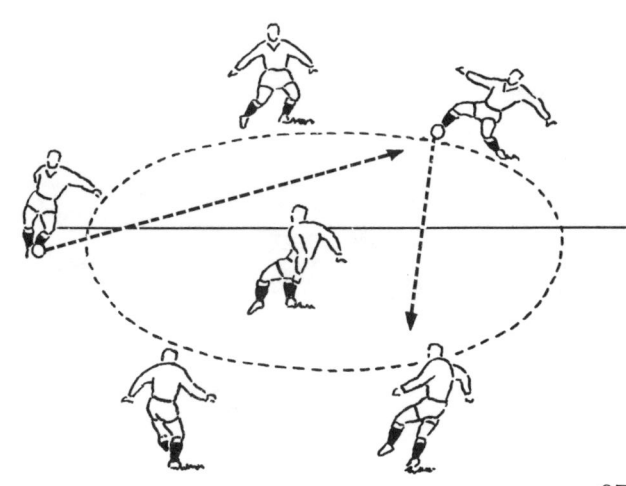

78 Shooting with Two Goals

Purpose:	Training for kick with the instep.
No. of players:	2 teams of 4–5.
Playing area:	Double penalty area, two normal goals, centre-line.
Duration:	30 mins. maximum.
Outline:	Each team must shoot goals from inside its own half. The players in possession try to work themselves into a good shooting position, while the opposition tries to block shots.
Rules:	The goalkeeper begins the game by throwing the ball out to a player in his team. If he is in a good position he may shoot immediately. If not, the ball may be passed directly to a team-mate. Three passes are the limit. No player may cross the centre-line. Balls out of play are either thrown or kicked back in.
Possible variations:	1. Change type of kick used (inside or outside of foot as well as instep). 2. Fix which foot to be used.
Remarks:	To improve the accuracy of the shooting, hockey goals can be used. In this case, all handling of the ball is forbidden.

79 Shooting with Common Goal

Purpose:	Training for kick with instep.
No. of players:	2 teams of 4–6 with 1 neutral goalkeeper.
Playing area:	Half the pitch, including normal goal.
Duration:	60 mins. maximum.
Outline:	One team attacks, trying to score goals, or to block shots if the other team is in possession.
Rules:	The game is started by the goalie kicking out randomly. A goal may not be scored unless one pass has been made. The other side gains possession by a succesful tackle, if the ball goes out of play, or after a foul. If the goalie gathers the ball, if it goes over the goal-line, or if a goal is scored, the game is restarted by a goal kick. No offside rule.
Possible variations:	1. Fix which foot to be used, and allow other kinds of shot. 2. Allow only first-time shots. 3. Goals scored only by headers.
Remarks:	This game is suitable for all ages and standards.

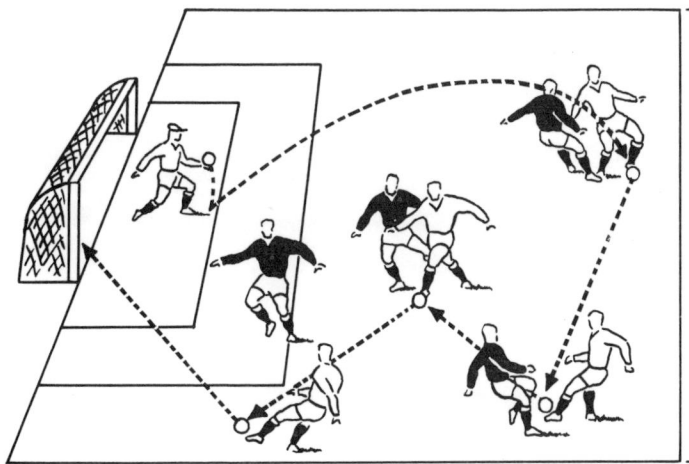

80 Shooting with Forbidden Area

Purpose:	Training for kick with the instep.
No. of players:	2 teams of 4. 1 neutral goalkeeper.
Playing area:	Half the pitch with a normal goal, and a shooting circle.
Duration:	60 mins. maximum.
Outline:	One team attacks, trying to score goals, or in defence to avoid conceding them.
Rules:	The game is started by a neutral goal kick. A goal may be scored only by a shot from outside the circle. If a player treads within the circle, the other team is awarded a free-kick from the same spot. No offside. No corner kicks. Balls rolling into the shooting circle go to the goalie. Outside this area or over the side-lines, balls are thrown in.
Possible variation:	Fix which foot to be used for shooting, and which other types of kick to be allowed.
Remarks:	The distance of the line marking the shooting limit to the goal should be adjusted to suit the ability of the players. For beginners the line should be no nearer than 8m., for skilled players a maximum of 18m.

81 Shooting From The Sides

Purpose:	Training for shot with the outside of foot.
No. of players:	2 teams of 4. 1 neutral goalkeeper.
Playing area:	Half the pitch with one normal goal. Shooting area marked by a line on which are flagposts, 5–12m. from the goal-line.
Duration:	30 mins. maximum.
Outline:	The team which has the ball tries to score goals by shooting from the permitted area between the flagpost and the goal-line. If the other team has the ball, they defend.
Rules:	The goalie starts the game with an impartial goal-kick. The team who manages to bring the ball under control tries to score goals from right or left side of the goal. Similarly for the other team. Fouls, infringement of the goal zone or shots from the wrong place are penalised by an indirect free-kick.
Possible variations:	1. Size of zone and position of flags may be varied. 2. One team may shoot only from the sides, the other only from between the flags.
Remarks:	For this game the basic techniques of shooting off the outside of the foot must be mastered.

82 Passing Back to Shoot

Purpose:	Training for kick with the instep.
No. of players:	2 teams of 4, one neutral goalkeeper.
Playing area:	Half the pitch, 1 normal goal.
Duration:	60 mins. maximum, or up to ten goals.
Outline:	One team attacks trying to score goals, or, having lost the ball, to avoid conceding goals.
Rules:	The goalie starts the game with an impartially taken goal-kick. A goal may be scored only after a pass back out of the penalty area. All players may use the penalty area. Shots from inside the penalty area are penalised by an indirect free-kick. No offside, but corners and throw-ins are taken. If the goalie gathers the ball, or if it goes over the goal-line, the game is restarted with a goal-kick. If a goal is scored, a goal-kick is also taken.
Possible variations:	1. Fix which foot to be used for shooting. 2. Allow further types of kick to be used.
Remarks:	Instead of using the penalty area, a "pass-back line" can be marked, at least 11m. out.

83   **Goal Shooting Starting From The Centre-Line**

Purpose:	Training for kick with the instep.
No. of players:	2 teams of 4, one neutral goalkeeper.
Playing area:	Half the pitch, one normal goal.
Duration:	50 mins. maximum.
Outline:	The attackers build up their moves from the centre-line and try to score goals, or, if the other team has the ball, try to block shots.
Rules:	The goalie starts the game with a kick. The team which wins the ball must first pass it back over the centre-line before they can mount an attack. After each completed attack the goalie restarts the game.
Possible variations:	1. Fix which foot to be used for shooting. 2. Put a time limit or the time allowed for the build up of the attack. 3. Limit number of times one team may play the ball consecutively.
Remarks:	It is recommended that players from different teams play against each other, to increase the competitive element and at the same time to rehearse set moves.

84 Obligatory Shooting

Purpose: Training for kick with instep.
No. of players: 2 teams of 2–5, one neutral goalie.
Playing area: Half the pitch, one normal goal.
Duration: 60 mins. maximum.
Outline: One team attacks and tries to score goals, or if in defence tries to avoid conceding goals.
Rules: The goalie starts the game with an impartial goal-kick. The ball is trapped and passed to a team-mate who is then obliged to shoot. Ball possession changes after interceptions, balls out of play, or errors in play (e.g. if it is not the second man who shoots), as well as after any foul. If the goalie gathers the ball or if it goes over the goal-line, he restarts the game with a goal-kick, as he does if a goal is scored.
Possible variation: Fix which foot and which type of kick to be used for shooting.
Remarks: If there are only two players on each side the first player must shoot. If more than four it's the third player.

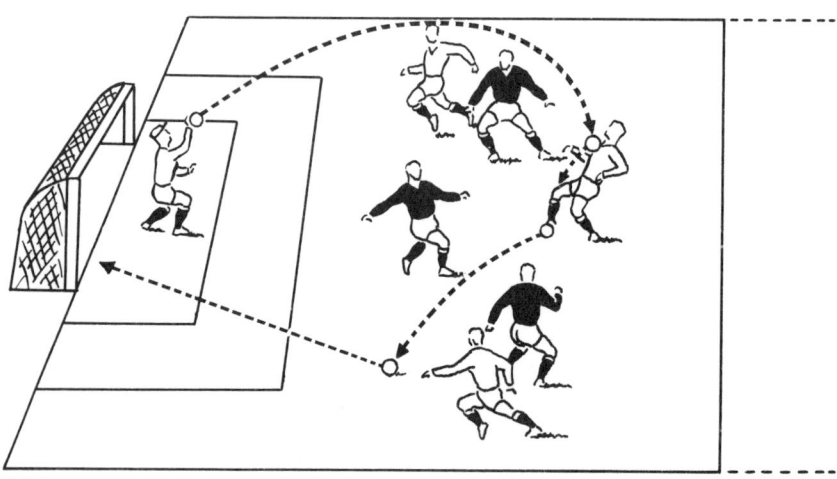

85   **Shooting with Medicine Ball as Target**

Purpose: Training for kick with instep.
No. of players: 2 teams of 3–7.
Playing area: 40 × 20m. Area divided into four zones by three parallel lines 10m. apart. One medicine ball on the centre-spot.
Duration: 25 mins. maximum.
Outline: Each team attempts to hit the medicine ball with hard, accurate shots, and to move it in the direction of the opposition. Each hit counts one point, but if a team manages to move the medicine ball over the 10m.-line they gain three points.
Rules: The players line up along the base-line, each with one ball. The medicine ball is on the centre-spot. On the whistle they shoot at the medicine ball. They may also use any ball the opposition kicks into their half.
Possible variations: 1. Vary types of kick used.
2. Ensure players are practising shots off both feet.
Remarks: It is worthwhile having a referee for each team.

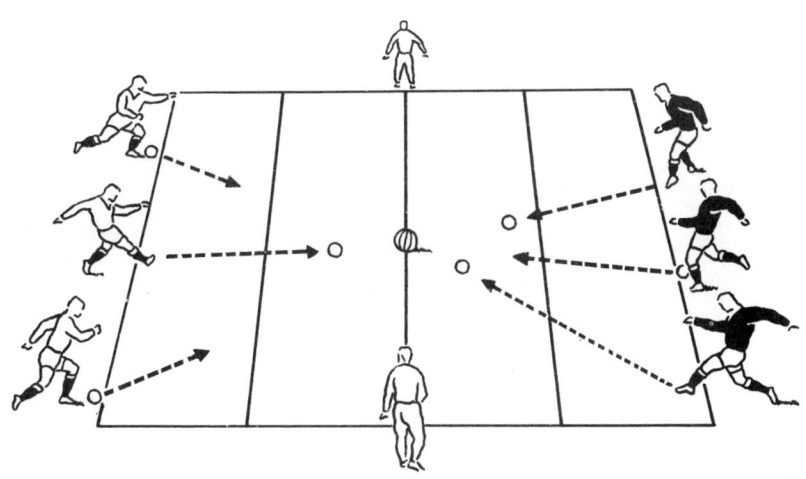

86 Shooting from Both Sides of one Goal

Purpose:	Training for kick with instep.
No. of players:	2 teams of 4, one neutral goalkeeper.
Playing area:	Unlimited; a goal 6 or 7m. wide in the middle.
Duration:	30 mins. maximum.
Outline:	One team attacks, trying to score goals, or, in defence, avoiding conceding goals.
Rules:	Goals may be scored from either side. If the ball passes through the flagposts, the game continues without interruption. If a shot goes above the posts it's no goal and the game carries on without a pause. If the goalie saves, he kicks out impartially. Balls out of play are thrown in.
Possible variations:	1. Fix which foot and which type if kick to be used for shooting. 2. Increase number of players to 6 v. 6.
Remarks:	It's a good idea to play two goalkeepers who alternate to share the high workload.

87 Shooting off Backboard

Purpose:	Training for kick with instep.
No. of players:	2 teams of 4.
Playing area:	30 × 20m. Two backboards on the base-lines, 6m. in front of these and facing them, hockey goals. In the gymnasium, use the walls as backboards.
Duration:	50 mins. maximum.
Outline:	Teams attempt to score goals—preferably by rebounds off the backboards—or, in defence, to avoid conceding goals.
Rules:	Teams attack the reversed goals. A goal is scored when the ball crosses the goal-line. The purpose of the game, however, is to score by rebound. These direct rebounds should count double or more. Handball or fouls are penalised by a direct free-kick against the backboard, which may not be defended. Goals scored from free-kicks score only one point.
Possible variation:	If the ball is in midfield, the trainer can change the goal which is to be attacked.
Remarks:	If goals are scored only rarely by rebounds, the defence should be banned from an area around the goal to limit their effectiveness.

88 Shooting Under the Rope

Purpose:	Training for kick with instep.
No. of players:	2 teams of 3–5.
Playing area:	30 × 15m. A 5m.-wide zone at either end, and a rope 1m. off the ground across the middle.
Duration:	20 mins. maximum.
Outline:	Each team takes up position in its 5m.-zone. Goals are scored by one team shooting under the rope and over the back line of the oppositions' area.
Rules:	Teams may not leave the 5m.-zone to shoot. Shots which hit the rope do not count. The man who stops the ball must take the next shot. Balls rebounding off the defence belong to the side which retrieves them first. The ball may be caught with the hands.
Possible variations:	1. Play with two or three balls. 2. First-time or only left- or right-footed shooting. 3. Vary the height of the rope.
Remarks:	Width of the area to be suited to the players' abilities. This game is particularly suitable for the gymnasium if it's of sufficient size.

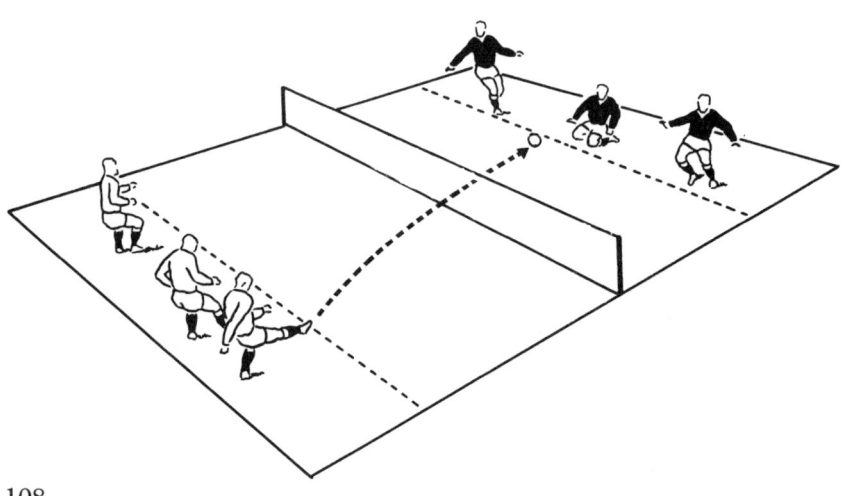

89 Free-Kick Competition

Purpose:	Training for kick with instep.
No. of players:	2 teams of 3–5, one neutral goalkeeper.
Playing area:	Roughly 70 × 30m., or one end of a pitch. 30m. out from the normal goal, a hockey goal.
Duration:	30 mins. maximum.
Outline:	The two teams take alternate shots from outside the penalty area at the normal goal, which is kept by the goalie. If a goal is scored, that team gets a bonus shot. If the goalie gathers a ball, he throws out to the other team, who then attack the small goal and can win an extra point by scoring in it.
Rules:	If the attack on the small goal is stopped or if the ball goes out of play, the other team is given possession and the free-kick game continues. Handling is not allowed by anyone in front of the small goal. For the free-kick game all players must take their turn.
Possible variations:	1. Fix which foot to be used. 2. Penalties may be substituted for free-kicks.

90 Three-Circle Game

Purpose:	Training for kick with instep.
No. of players:	Unlimited. Each game 1 *v.* 1.
Playing area:	40 × 20m., three circles in each half. One circle 10m. from the centre-line, the others about 15m. away. Circles of about 3m. diameter.
Duration:	20 mins. maximum, or up to 20 points.
Outline:	Each player tries to kick the ball from a circle in his own half into one of the circles in the opposing half. If the shot succeeds, it counts one point.
Rules:	Points are scored only by shots which land directly in the circle. For shots which do not cross the centre-line or land out of play, one point is deducted. Shots may not be taken consecutively from the same circle.
Possible variations:	1. The other player can save points by intercepting the ball before it hits the circle. Handball not allowed. 2. Shots taken on the volley which hit an opponent's circle count double.
Remarks:	Make sure circles are clearly marked (perhaps also with flags etc.).

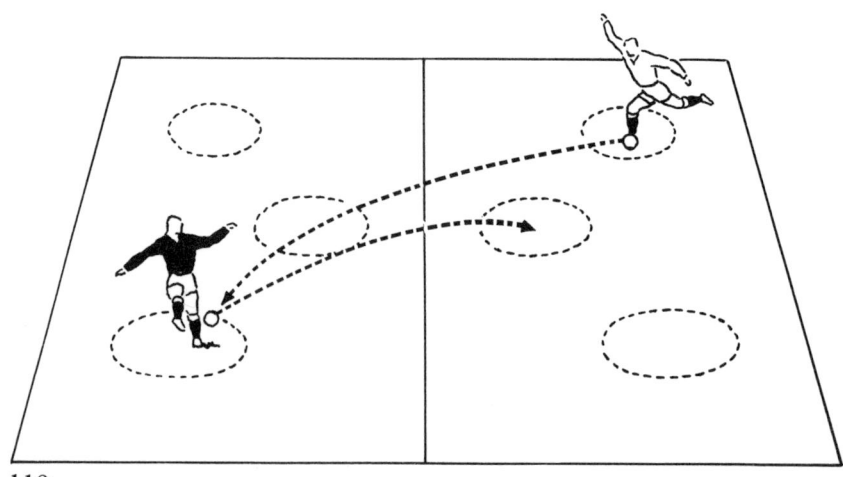

91 Game With No Midfield

Purpose: Training for kick with instep.
No. of players: 2 teams of 5.
Playing area: 40 × 20m., two hockey goals facing outwards.
Duration: 40 mins. maximum.
Outline: The team in possession attacks its opponents' goal. Goals can be scored only after they have been passed across the midfield area, in which the ball must not bounce.
Rules: One team begins the game in its own goalmouth. The ball must be passed right across the midfield before a shot at goal can be made. If the ball does land in midfield, the opposition takes a throw-in from the point where the ball crossed the sideline. Players may run across the midfield. The last defender may handle the ball.
Possible variations: 1. Increase the width of the midfield, and the number of players to 7 *v.* 7. No handling allowed.
2. Midfield may be crossed by a player with the ball as long as he keeps it in the air. If it bounces, a free-kick is given to the opposition from the spot where it lands.

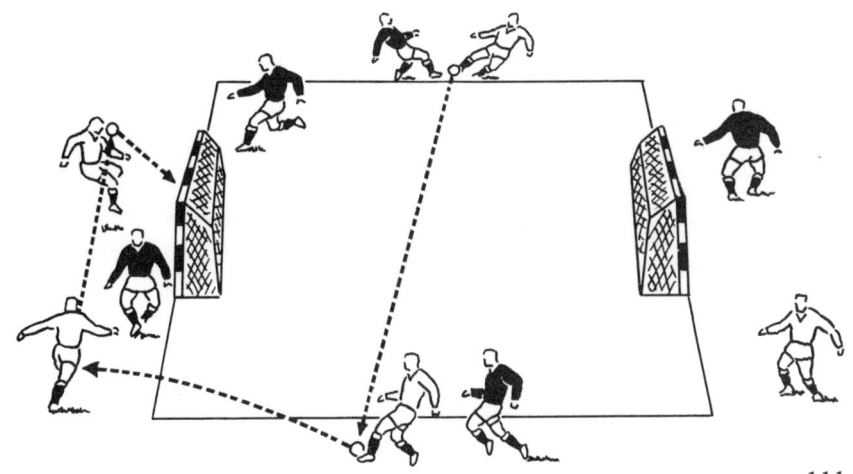

92   Treble Target

Purpose:	Training for kick with instep.
No. of players:	Unlimited. Each game 1 v. 1.
Playing area:	40 × 10m., 6 lines across the area, 4m., 7m. and 10m. from either end.
Duration:	30 mins. maximum.
Outline:	Players attempt to kick the ball from the zone in their own half into the same zone in their opponents' half, thereby scoring points. They can be worth different amounts: Zone I to zone I (20–26m.) 1 pt. Zone II to zone II (26–32m.) 2 pts. Zone III to zone III (32–40m.) 3 pts.
Rules:	Only shots landing direct into the target area score. After a given period of time points are totalled up and the winner declared.
Possible variations:	1. Volleyed shots count double. 2. Minimum 10 shots to be made from each zone.
Remarks:	Ensure both feet are used. Ensure zones are clearly marked (perhaps additional markers, e.g. flagposts on the sidelines).

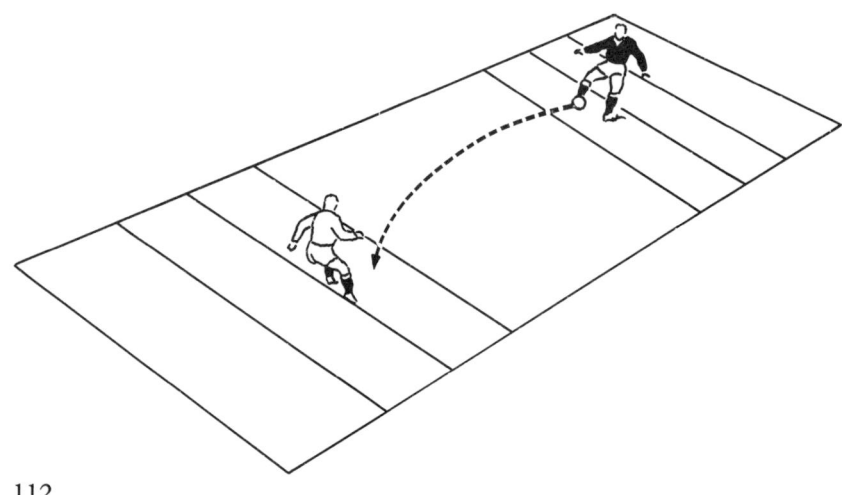

93   Kicking for Distance

Purpose:	Training for long kick with instep.
No. of players:	8, 4 *v.* 4.
Playing area:	Whole pitch.
Duration:	25 mins. maximum.
Outline:	Each team tries to drive its opponents back to their base-line by long kicks. A point is scored when the ball lands behind the goal-line.
Rules:	Teams line up at an equal distance on either side of the centre-line. One team kicks off as far as it can towards the opposing goal-line. Where the ball lands it is placed and kicked back as far as possible by the opposition.
Possible variations:	1. Increase number of players, but then introduce volleyed returns. 2. Balls headed before they land gain 5m. advantage.
Remarks:	Players should return the ball in strictly numerical order.

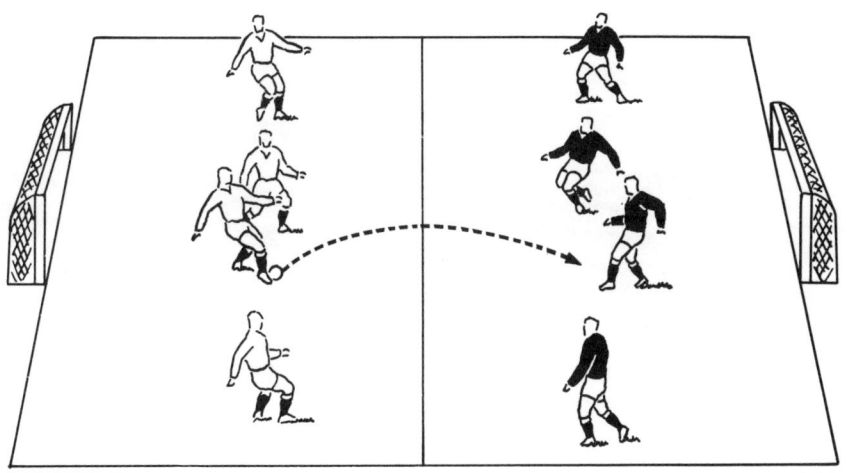

94 High Target

Purpose:	Training for kick with instep.
No. of players:	2 teams of an unlimited number.
Playing area:	40 × 15m., two vaulting boxes in the middle, each with a medicine ball on them.
Duration:	40 mins. maximum.
Outline:	Teams try to score points by hitting the medicine ball from behind their base-line. Every player has one ball. Each hit counts one point.
Rules:	Points are scored only when the medicine ball is hit direct. If the medicine ball falls off due to the impact of the ball against the box, no point is scored. In this case the ball must be replaced by the team who knocked it off. If the medicine ball is hit directly, it must be replaced by the other team. Teams must stay behind their line.
Possible variations:	1. Shots to be made with both feet. 2. Vary type of kick to be used. 3. Increase distance from line to horse to 30m.
Remarks:	It is advisable to have two referees, one for each team.

95 Relay With Long Cross Passes

Purpose:	Training for long pass with instep.
No. of players:	2 teams of unlimited numbers.
Playing area:	Normal pitch, two lines from each corner of the penalty area.
Duration:	10 sprints per player.
Outline:	Each player in a team can score one point by dribbling the ball up to the centre line and giving a long pass with the instep across to the far corner to his team-mate.
Rules:	Half of each team line up at either diagonally opposite corner. Each team has one ball. On the word go, the first players of each team dribble the ball towards the centre. From there they give a long lofted cross to the far corner, run across after it and line up at the back of their team. The next player of this group then starts. The game finishes when all players are back in their original positions. Passes must land directly in the marked corner.
Possible variations:	1. The winner is the first team to finish. 2. Change sides after each game.
Remarks:	Particularly suitable for players with a good standard of accuracy.

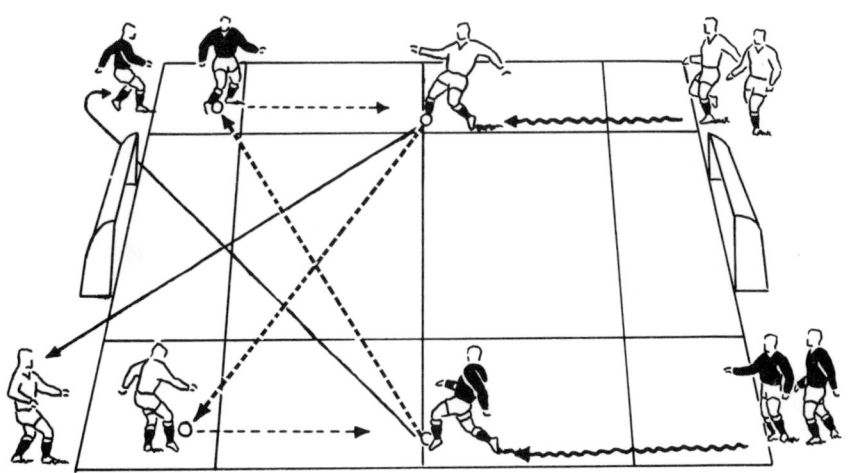

96 Dribbling: Six-Zone Game

Purpose:	Dribbling practice.
No. of players:	2 teams of 6.
Playing area:	60 × 20m. divided into six equal zones of 20 × 10m.
Duration:	10 attacks per team, maximum.
Outline:	One team attacks, the other defends. Members of the attacking side each have a ball. A point is awarded to any player who can dribble the ball through the defence and over the goal-line. The defence line up in alternate zones, 3 in the front, 2 in the middle and one in the back zone. They try to rob the attackers of the ball.
Rules:	On the word go, the attack starts. Any player who is dispossessed or forced into touch drops out of the attack. Defenders are not allowed to leave their zone. In the unoccupied zones the attack can regroup for the next assault. After each round, the teams change places. The winner is announced after all the rounds are finished.
Remarks:	Ensure that players tackle fairly, to avoid any injuries resulting from the one-to-one situation.

97   Dribbling: Advancing in Stages

Purpose:	Dribbling practice.
No. of players:	2 teams of 6–8.
Playing area:	Normal pitch divided into four equal zones the width of the pitch.
Duration:	60 mins. maximum.
Outline:	One team attacks, the other defends. The attack must capture opposition territory by dribbling the ball across the lines.
Rules:	One team starts off in their own half. If they manage a breakthrough into the next zone they can use all that territory as theirs. A goal may be scored only if the shot is made from the zone directly in front of the goal.
	Ball possession changes if the opposition intercepts successfully, if the ball goes out of play or if the ball is passed, rather than dribbled over a line. Proper goalkeepers, but no offside rule. Goalies may take part in their team's attacks.
Possible variation:	Encourage players to use various dribbling techniques.
Remarks:	Particularly suitable for those players who have mastered the basics of ball control.

98 Dribbling into Shooting Area

Purpose:	Dribbling practice.
No. of players:	2 teams of 6.
Playing area:	Crosswise in one half, with a hockey goal at either end, and a shooting circle of 12–20m. radius.
Duration:	40 mins. maximum.
Outline:	One team tries to dribble the ball into the opponents' shooting area and then to score goals. In front of their own goal, the defence attempt to stop the opposition scoring.
Rules:	One team attacks. They may score goals only when one team member succeeds in dribbling the ball into the shooting circle; once there, the goal may come as a result of good combination play. Shots from outside the circle do not count and are penalised by a free-kick.
Possible variations:	1. Vary method of dribbling to be used. 2. Vary number of players and size of playing area. 3. Use the various techniques employed in similar games (e.g. only low passing, only left-footed shots etc.).
Remarks:	The size of the circle should be reduced if the players are of above average skills.

Dribbling: Four-Zone Game

Purpose:	Dribbling practice.
No. of players:	Groups of 4.
Playing area:	32 × 10m., divided into four zones of 8 × 10m.
Duration:	20 mins. maximum.
Outline:	One player attempts to dribble round three others consecutively. For each man he beats, he receives one point. The winner is the player with most points.
Rules:	One player stands on each of the three middle lines. The dribbler starts off with the ball at his feet, trying to go round his three opponents one after the other. If he loses the ball, he gains no points, but retains the ball and carries on to the next defender.
Defenders must remain on their lines. After each man has dribbled over the end line, players all move forward one line and the next man takes his turn.
Possible variations:	1. Defenders to stay not only on their line but within their whole zone.
2. Size of area and number of players may be varied.
Remarks:	This game is better suited to well trained and technically skilled players.

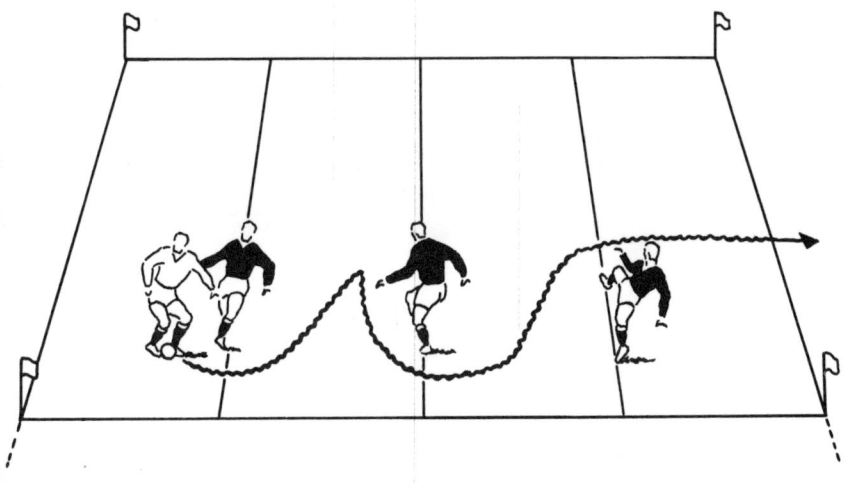

100 Open-Goal Game

Purpose: Dribbling practice.
No. of players: Any number of pairs.
Playing area: 20 × 20m. A 2m.-wide goal (flags as goalposts) and around it a circle with a diameter of 5m.
Duration: 5 × 2 mins.
Outline: One player attempts to dribble round his opponent and score.
Rules: The player in possession tries to dribble past his opponent and then to score goals. After each goal is scored, the other man is given the ball. If a successful tackle is made or the ball goes into touch, the opponent becomes attacker. Deflected or opportunist goals are not allowed. For this reason the ball must be outside the 5m. circle before the next attack can begin.
Possible variations: 1. The 5m. circle may not be entered, ten markings acting as a shooting limit.
2. Vary method used for dribbling.
Remarks: During the pauses it's a good idea to make the players practise ball-skills.

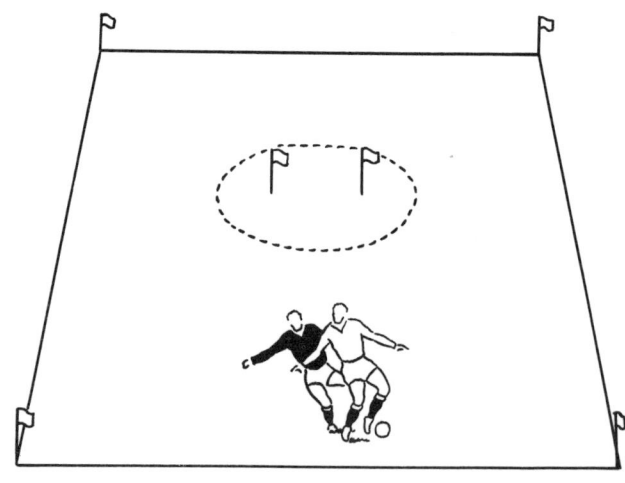

101   Dribbling the Ball over the Line

Purpose: Dribbling practice.
No. of players: 10–12, 5 *v.* 5 or 6 *v.* 6.
Playing area: Across one half of a normal pitch.
Duration: 30 mins. maximum.
Outline: Teams try to combine so as to set one player free to dribble the ball over the opposition goal-line and score. The winner is the team with most goals after a given time.
Rules: No proper goalkeepers, no offside rule. If ball possession is lost, the other team continues the game. The whole back line counts as a goal-line. The opposition take the ball each time a goal is scored.
Possible variations: 1. Fix which foot to be used for dribbling.
2. Fix which method to be used for dribbling (e.g. inside or outside of foot).

102 Dribbling Touch

Purpose:	Dribbling practice.
No. of players:	2 teams of 4–8.
Playing area:	Penalty area, divided into halves.
Duration:	20 mins. maximum.
Outline:	Each team have one half of the pitch and each player has a ball. One player from each side plays in the opposing half, with the object of touching as many players as he can but without losing control of his own ball.
Rules:	One point for every player touched, or if any opposition player loses control over his ball, or dribbles out of play. If the chaser loses control of his, then he drops out and is replaced by another member of his team. After all members of the teams have been chaser, the winner is announced. Two referees are necessary for this game to observe the results of the chaser in each half.
Possible variations:	1. Time limit of 2–4 mins. for each chaser. 2. Fix which foot and/or method to be used for dribbling.

103 Two Too Few

Purpose:	Dribbling practice.
No. of players:	2 teams of 4–6.
Playing area:	40 × 20m. with a marked centre-line.
Duration:	20 sprints per man.
Outline:	Teams line up opposite each other on the shorter sides of the area. On the middle line are two balls less than the total number of players (six balls for eight players, ten for twelve etc.). On the word "go" both teams sprint towards the balls and retrieve as many as they can, dribbling them back to their line. One point for every ball retrieved.
Rules:	Those two players who are unable to find a spare ball try to kick away as many balls from their opponents' feet as they can. Balls kicked out of play are lost; balls crossing the goal-line count one point for that team. The important thing is that the players should dribble the ball across their line. Balls just kicked over it do not count.
Possible variation:	Fix method to be used.
Remarks:	One referee for each half of the field is preferable.

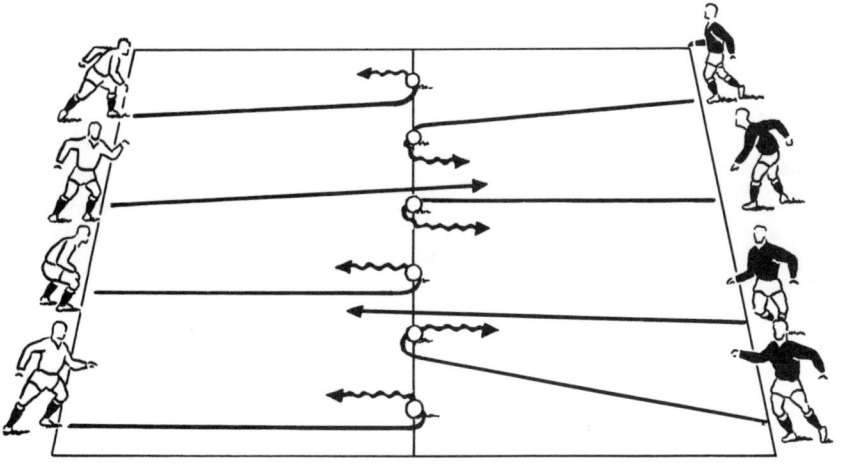

104   Dribbling: Zone Changing

Purpose:	Dribbling practice.
No. of players:	2 teams of 4–6.
Playing area:	Half pitch with equal zones. Always one zone more than the number of players in one team (4 players = 5 zones etc.).
Duration:	40 mins. maximum.
Outline:	One team attacks and tries to score goals, the other team defends. If a player receives the ball in a free zone, he may run with the ball without being tackled.
Rules:	When changing zones the ball must be dribbled across the dividing line, at which time the opposition may challenge him again. Playing right across a free zone is not allowed. A shot at goal may be made only after a zone-change. No proper goalkeepers, but the last defender of either team may handle the ball. Throw-ins and corners are taken. No offside.
Possible variation:	Fix method and foot to be used.
Remarks:	Adapt size of area and duration of game to the players' capabilities.

105 Dribbling: Four Quarters

Purpose:	Dribbling practice.
No. of players:	2 teams of 4.
Playing area:	20 × 20m., area quartered.
Duration:	20 mins. maximum.
Outline:	The four quarters of the area are numbered. One member of each team in one quarter. If a team can manage to pass in turn 1–2–3–4 without losing the ball, it receives one point.
Rules:	Players are restricted to their own quarters. If a player intercepts, the game continues clockwise, and this team likewise win one point after three more passes. Similarly, if the ball goes out of play, when players run over the line, or if a foul is committed, the opposition is given the ball.
Possible variations:	1. Vary the technique to be used for dribbling. 2. Play with no direction, with one point for each successful pass.
Remarks:	The less skilful the players, the bigger the area should be.

106	**Dribbling Relay Round the Centre Circle**
Purpose:	Dribbling practice.
No. of players:	2 teams of equal numbers.
Playing area:	Centre-circle, including centre-line.
Duration:	20 mins. maximum or ten runs per team.
Outline:	Members of a team must dribble the ball round the circle. The ball is given to the next man after each complete circuit. The first team to finish wins.
Rules:	On the word "go" the first men start their run round the circle from the point where the centre-line cuts the circle; on arriving back at the line they pass the ball on to the next man. After all the players have had their turn, one run is finished. If man or ball enters the circle, the team is disqualified.
Possible variations:	1. Vary dribbling technique. 2. Each player has a ball—all start simultaneously. 3. Several turns to be taken consecutively.
Remarks:	Adapt strenuousness of game to fitness level of players.

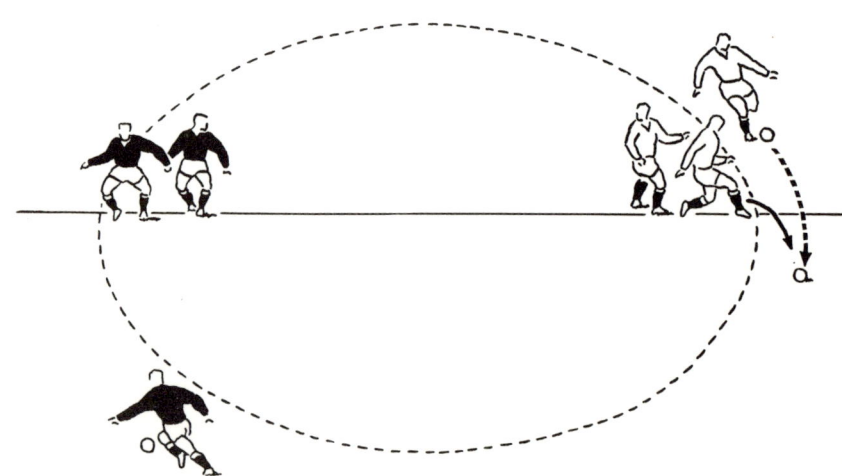

107 Slalom Relay

Purpose:	Dribbling practice.
No. of players:	2 teams of equal numbers.
Playing area:	Starting line with two lines of flagposts about 2m. apart.
Duration:	20 mins. maximum or ten runs per team.
Outline:	Each player of a team must dribble the ball in between all the flagposts both out and back in a shorter time than the player from the opposing team, to win one point.
Rules:	On the word "go" the first men of each team start dribbling. The next man can go only when the first player passes him the ball over the starting line. The team to finish first is awarded one point. A flying start means the whole team's disqualification.
Possible variations:	1. Vary dribbling technique to be used. 2. If flagposts are placed at uneven distances the dribbling is made more difficult.
Remarks:	Suitable for all ages and standards.

108 Simple Heading Game

Purpose:	Heading practice.
No. of players:	1 v. 1.
Playing area:	10–16m. × 5 × 8m. Centre-line to be marked. Flagposts at each corner.
Duration:	20 mins. maximum, or up to 10 goals, including change of ends.
Outline:	The players try to head the ball over their opponent's goal-line and score points. The winner is the man with the most points after a given length of time.
Rules:	Start the heading by tossing the ball up. The player who starts can head the ball several times consecutively up to the centre-line from where he can head a shot. Neither player may cross the centre-line. Direct shots are allowed. If a player loses control of the ball, a free shot (with the head) is given from the centre.
Possible variations:	1. No centre-line; the ball may be headed as far as desired, but the ball can be punched away at any time by the opponent. 2. Several pairs play simultaneously, a knock-out competition is organized.
Remarks:	This game is suitable for all ages and standards. Adapt the size of area and duration of play to the stamina of the players.

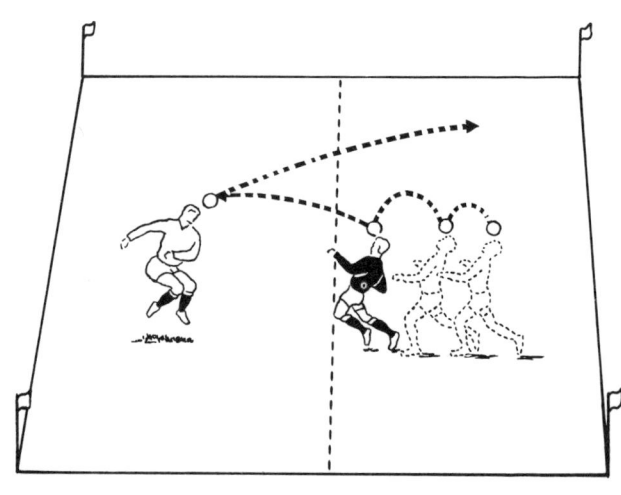

109 Headers in Pairs

Purpose:	Heading practice.
No. of players:	2 v. 2.
Playing area:	16 × 8m. Marked centre-line, flags for goalposts.
Duration:	20 mins. maximum, or up to 10 goals, including change of ends.
Outline:	Each pair try to head the ball over the opponents' goal-line to score.
Rules:	Start the heading by tossing the ball up. To get into a good shooting position, the players may head the ball as often as they wish but they may not cross the centre-line. If the ball hits the ground, the other pair receives a free shot from the centre.
Possible variations:	1. No centre-line. 2. The ball may be punched away by the opposition anywhere on the field.
Remarks:	This game is suitable for all ages and standards. Adapt the size of area and duration of play to the stamina of the players.

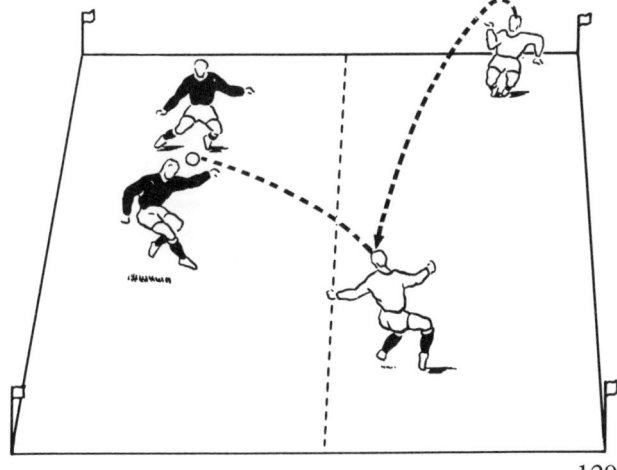

110   Heading from a Midfield Pass

Purpose:	Heading practice.
No. of players:	8. 4 v. 4, two from each team in midfield and 1 at each end as attack and defence.
Playing area:	30 × 15m. Two outwards-facing hockey goals. Centre-line.
Duration:	35 mins. maximum. Change of positions with short pause every 5 minutes.
Outline:	One team attacks the opposition half and tries to score goals, or, if the ball is lost, tries to stop the other team scoring.
Rules:	A goal can be scored only off a direct throw from inside the attacking half. In midfield the ball must be passed with the hands, but in front of the goals only the head may be used. If possession is lost, the opponents continue to attack. The players positioned in front of the goal must do some fast and clever running off the ball to be able to head goals for their team.
Remarks:	An imporant part of this game is the passing of the ball. Whereas less skilled players should be allowed to let the ball bounce, direct passing should be the rule for skilled players. The duration of the game and number of goals to be scored should be adapted to the players' stamina.

111 Headers with Four Neutral Players

Purpose:	Heading practice.
No. of players:	2 v. 2 and four neutral players.
Playing area:	40 × 20m. Two hockey goals.
Duration:	40 mins. maximum.
Outline:	Two players defend their goal. The other two attack, trying to score. The four neutrals are always on the attacking side.
Rules:	One player begins by heading the ball to his partner or to one of the four. The ball may be played only with the head. If the ball hits the ground or is intercepted by one of the two defenders, the play switches over. If the ball goes over the touchline, it is headed in from the same point.
Possible variation:	Limit number of consecutive headers allowed.
Remarks:	Particularly suitable for those age-levels and standards where the players have mastered the basics of heading technique. For skilled players, use less neutral players; for unskilled, more.

112 Headers: Handball Game with no Shooting-Circle

Purpose: Heading practice.
No. of players: 2 teams of 4–7.
Playing area: 40 × 20m., two hockey goals.
Duration: 40 mins. maximum.
Outline: One team defends its goal, the other attacks until a goal is scored or ball-possession is lost.
Rules: One team begins the game by throwing the ball in. Goals may be scored only by a header from a direct pass. The man holding the ball cannot score himself. If ball-possession is lost, the opposing side continues the attack. A throw-in is given if the ball goes out of play. No offside, no proper goalkeeper. Any member of the team can defend the goal and handle the ball.
Possible variations: 1. To make goal-scoring easier, use full-size goals.
2. Mark a line 10m. out from the goal and allow a maximum of three players behind it.
Remarks: This game, if adapted, is suitable for all ages and standards.

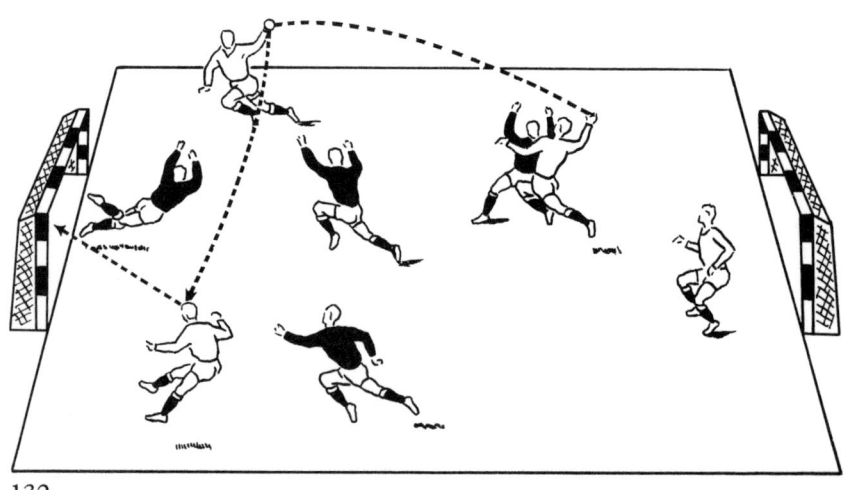

113 Headers: Full Game

Purpose:	Heading practice.
No. of players:	2 teams of 5–7.
Playing area:	40 × 20m., two hockey goals.
Duration:	40 mins. maximum.
Outline:	One team defends its goal; the other attacks until a goal is scored or possession is lost. The team who has scored most goals over a given period of time is the winner.
Rules:	The game is started by the ball being thrown into the air. Only the head may be used; catching the ball in the air is not allowed. Only when the ball has bounced can it be picked up and the game continued by the team first to the loose ball. Any infringement is penalised by a free header; similarly if the ball goes into touch.
Possible variation:	Stipulate beforehand if the man in possession can score himself or whether a goal may be scored only direct from a pass.
Remarks:	For the more skilful teams it is possible to play 3 v. 3 or 4 v. 4, if the playing area is reduced to 25 × 20m.

114 Headers: Distance Game

Purpose:	Heading practice.
No. of players:	2 teams of 3–5.
Playing area:	20m. wide strip across normal pitch.
Duration:	20 mins. maximum.
Outline:	Teams try to score goals by forcing their opponents back and themselves forward and heading the ball over the goal-line.
Rules:	One team begins by heading the ball, from behind the centre-line into the other half. If the ball is caught in mid-air the catcher may take one pace forward and head the ball back. Otherwise the ball is headed from the spot where it is picked up. Direct returns are allowed. If the ball goes into touch, game is recontinued from the spot it left the field. The catcher of the ball must always be the one to head it.
Remarks:	Adapt the dimensions of the playing area to the capabilities of the players. The exercise is more effective with smaller groups in which each player heads the ball frequently.

115 Headers: Tennis

Purpose:	Heading practice.
No. of players:	2 teams of 6–8.
Playing area:	18 × 9m. (as volleyball court). Across the middle a net or a rope 1.50m. high.
Duration:	Best of three sets of 20 points. If scores are level after two games a decider is played in which teams change ends after 10 points.
Outline:	The ball must be headed over the net into the opposition half, and may bounce only once. Only the team on serve can score.
Rules:	The game is started by one player heading towards his opponents from his own half. The receiver can let the service bounce once before returning it or return directly. The ball may be headed among members of a team as many times as is needed. After every fault the ball is served again, each time by a different player. Preferably the ball should be served by the head, but it is possible to alter this rule for a long game to allow the serve to be made by kneeing or kicking the ball. A fault occurs as follows:
	(a) If the service is not allowed to bounce in the receiver's court.
	(b) If the ball bounces more than once.
	(c) If the ball is headed into the net.
	(d) If the ball is headed over the boundary of the court.
	(e) If the ball is played other than with the head.
	(f) If a player enters the opponents' court.
Possible variations:	1. Return of ball to be made directly.
	2. Interpassing in one team may be made with the feet, but the return over the net with the head only.
	3. The number of players can be varied according to their age and fitness.

Remarks: The centre-circle of a football pitch also makes a suitable court. In practice, the game goes better with a lighter ball, e.g. volleyball, plastic football, etc., which demands quicker reactions on the part of the players because of its bounciness.

116   **Headers: Volleyball**

Purpose:	Heading practice.
No. of players:	2 teams of 6–8.
Playing area:	18 × 9m. (volleyball court). Across the middle a net 2.40m. high.
Duration:	Best of three sets of 20 points.
Outline:	The ball must be headed over the net and may not touch the ground. Only the team on service can score.
Rules:	The game is started by a player heading the ball over the net from anywhere within his own half. The ball may not bounce but can be played four times within one team. The return may be made by any member of the team. Each team has five consecutive services, each by a different player. Service is taken after every fault.

A fault occurs when:

(a) the ball touches the net on the serve.

(b) the ball lands outside the court.

(c) the ball touches the ground.

	(d) more than four consecutive headers are made by one team.
	(e) the ball is played other than with the head.
	(f) if one player plays the ball more than once consecutively.
Possible variations:	1. Service to be taken from behind the base-line.
	2. Allow more than four headers before the return.
	3. Each member of the team to head the ball before it is returned.
Remarks:	The basics of heading technique must already be familiar to players of this game.

117 Headers: Through Rings

Purpose:	Heading practice.
No. of players:	2 teams of 4–6.
Playing area:	Gymnasium. Several rings suspended from the ceiling of about 1m. diameter and at least 1m. above head height.
Duration:	30 mins. maximum.
Outline:	A team is awarded one point if a player manages to head the ball through one of the rings. Balls headed through after a player has thrown the ball up himself count one point, but double if they are headed direct from a pass.
Rules:	Passing within a team is done with the hands, as in handball or basketball. Any player may score. The wallbars count as "cushions", i.e. play is not interrupted. After a goal is scored, play continues without pause.
Possible variation:	Increase height of the rings to make the game more difficult.
Remarks:	The diameter of the rings must be suited to the skills of the players, but a minimum diameter of 80cm. is advisable. This game can be played on grass, if stands can be found for the rings.

118 Throw-in Game

Purpose: Throw-in training.
No. of players: 2 teams of five.
Playing area: 40 × 20m.
Duration: 30 mins. maximum.
Outline: Teams try to attack the opposition goal by skilful positioning and to win points. The passing of the ball and scoring of goals are done by legal "throw-ins".
Rules: One team starts the game. The ball may be thrown only when both hands are behind the head and both feet firmly on the ground. Players may not move when they have the ball. The opposition gets the ball if an interception is made, if the ball goes out of play or is played with the feet. Corners are thrown in. No proper goalkeepers, no offside.
Possible variations: 1. Chalk out a shooting circle of about 10m. diameter.
2. Use normal size goals with a goalkeeper.
Remarks: Suitable for all ages and standards.

119 Throw-in: Moving Targets

Purpose:	Throw-in training.
No. of players:	3 teams of 4–6.
Playing area:	30 × 20m. divided into three zones; the middle one may be larger than the outside zones.
Duration:	20 mins. maximum.
Outline:	Each team has its own zone. The players in the outside zones try to hit those in the middle with the ball. Only balls that are thrown as for a legal throw-in count.
Rules:	The ball may be passed a maximum of twice within one team. The teams in the outside zones try to hit the middle men. The players in the middle team are not allowed to catch the ball and may protect themselves only by avoiding the shot. After five attempts, the middle team change over with one of those on the outside. When a man has been hit, the ball is given back to the team who made the successful shot.
Possible variation:	Several balls may be used.
Remarks:	For training the long throw-in, the length of the zones can be increased.

120   Throwing-in Long Shots

Purpose:	Throw-in training.
No. of players:	2 teams of 2.
Playing area:	Normal soccer pitch.
Duration:	15 mins. maximum.
Outline:	Players attempt to throw the ball over their opponents making ground and finally reaching the goal-line, for which one point is awarded.
Rules:	Teams line up opposite each other at equal distance from centre-line. One player starts the game by throwing the ball over the heads of the opposing players. The ball is returned in the same way from the spot where the other team stops it.
Possible variations:	1. After each score, pairs are changed. 2. The ball may be returned from the spot where it landed.
Remarks:	Pay attention that the ball is thrown in a correct and legal manner.

121 Throwing-in at Opposition

Purpose: Throw-in training.
No. of players: 2 teams of 6–8.
Playing area: 20 × 10m., divided into halves by a centre-line.
Duration: 20 mins. maximum.
Outline: Teams line up in their own halves but with one man positioned behind the opponents' goal-line. The team in possession tries to hit their opponents with the ball by passing the ball about, using throw-ins. The winner is declared when all the members of one team have been hit.

Rules: Players who have been hit retire behind the opponents' goal-line. These players can throw the ball at their opponents at any time, and if their shot is good they may return to midfield. Those players in the field of play may aim a shot only if they catch the ball in their half. Ball possession changes if the ball can be caught clearly by the player being aimed at.

Remarks: To train for the long throw, the size of the area can be increased.
To strengthen the trunk muscles, the game can be played with a heavy medicine ball.

122 Double-Zone Game

Purpose:	Tackling training.
No. of players:	2 teams of 5.
Playing area:	40 × 20m. with centre-line. A 2m.-wide goal at either end.
Duration:	25 mins. maximum.
Outline:	Each team is composed of three attackers and two defenders. The attackers try to score goals and the defenders to stop the opposition scoring.
Rules:	The attackers stand in the opposition half, the defenders in their own half, so that a three against two situation in front of goal always occurs. No player may cross the centre-line. If the defence wins the ball, if it goes out of play, or if there is any infringement of the rules, the other attackers are given the ball.
Possible variation:	Limit the number of passes the attack may make before shooting, or impose a time-limit.
Remarks:	Attackers and defenders must change positions at regular intervals. The game can also be played in small gymnasiums, using the walls as cushions.

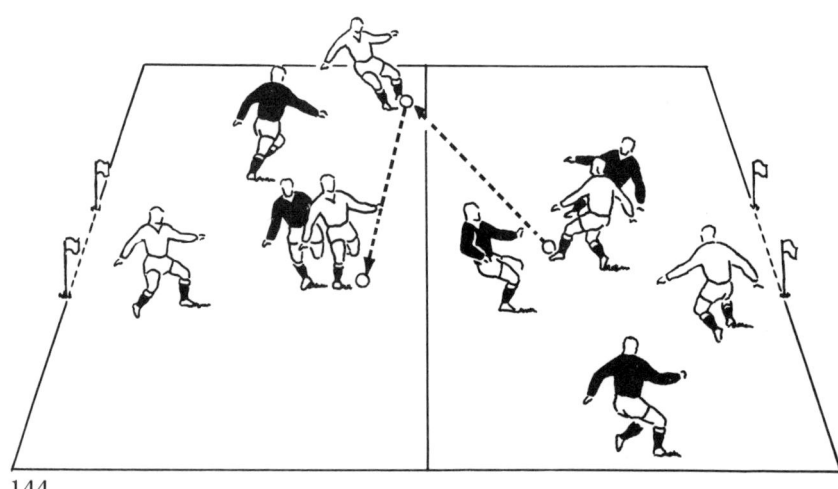

Games for tactical training

123 Numbers Passing Game

Purpose:	Training for running off the ball and covering.
No. of players:	2 teams of 4–7.
Playing area:	Half a normal pitch. No goal.
Duration:	30 mins. maximum.
Outline:	Teams play the ball in numerical order, trying to score points.
Rules:	Each team has distinctive jerseys, numbered consecutively. One team starts the game at No. 1 and is awarded one point if the ball is passed through the team in the correct order without being intercepted by the opposition. The opposition receives the ball when the sequence is completed, if they make an interception, if a foul is committed or the ball goes out of play.
Possible variations:	1. Whoever intercepts the ball can pass the ball to the man one number higher, without having to give it first to No. 1. 2. Limit the number of times ball may be played before the pass.
Remarks:	It's worthwhile pairing off players, 1 with 1, 2 with 2 etc., to avoid the whole team blocking the next player in the sequence.

124   Game with Captains

Purpose:	Training for running off the ball and covering.
No. of players:	2 teams of 4–6.
Playing area:	Half a normal pitch.
Duration:	20 mins. maximum.
Outline:	Teams elect a captain. When a team manages to pass the ball to its captain, it is awarded one point.
Rules:	One team starts trying to pass the ball to its captain. The other team puts its effort into preventing this, and to winning the ball. If the opposition manages to intercept, or if the ball goes out of play, or if a point is scored, it is given the ball. Captains are switched after a certain time, depending on their stamina, since it is they who have to run most.
Possible variation:	The team who wins one point retains the ball and continues the game.
Remarks:	The captains of each team should be clearly recognizable (cap, special jersey etc.).

125 Three Against One

Purpose:	Training for running off the ball and covering.
No. of players:	4, 3 *v.* 1.
Playing area:	10 × 10m.
Duration:	20 mins. maximum.
Outline:	The three players must pass among themselves. The single player tries to intercept their passes by skilful positioning.
Rules:	The three players begin the game by passing among themselves. The sequence is broken only if the defender touches the ball, if it goes out of play or if the ball is passed above head height. In these cases the single player changes over with the man who last played the ball.
Possible variation:	Limit the number of times the ball may be played.
Remarks:	The running off the ball is being done correctly when the player who has the ball has two opportunities to pass, i.e. when neither of the two others is covered by the one defender. For less skilled players this game should be first practised on a larger area (20 × 20m.).

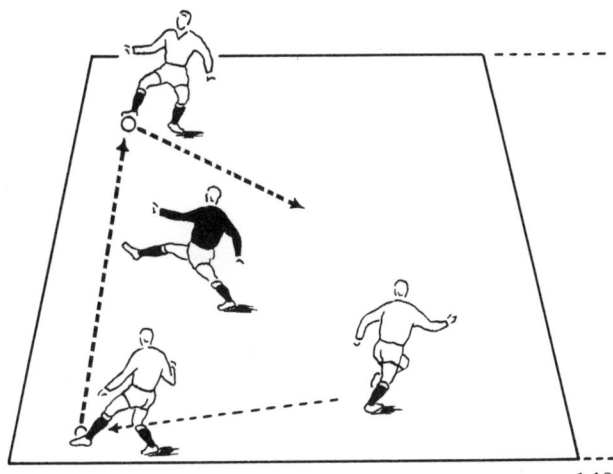

126 Four against Two

Purpose:	Training for running off the ball and covering.
No. of players:	6. 4 v. 2.
Playing area:	25 × 25m.
Duration:	30 mins. maximum.
Outline:	The four players must pass the ball among themselves. The two defenders try to intercept their passes by skilful positioning.
Rules:	The team of four begins the game by passing among themselves. The sequence is broken only if the defenders touch the ball, if it goes out of play or if the ball is passed above head height. In these cases the player who last touches the ball changes with one of the defenders. Otherwise changes can be made on a rota basis.
Possible variations:	1. Players may play the ball an unlimited number of times. 2. Players may play the ball twice only. 3. First-time passing.
Remarks:	Running off the ball is being done correctly when the player with the ball has three opportunities of passing. For skilled footballers the playing area can be reduced to 16.50 × 15m.

127 Two against One

Purpose:	Training for running off the ball and covering.
No. of players:	3. 2 v. 1.
Playing area:	16.50 × 15m.
Duration:	4 × 5 mins., with intervals of up to 3 mins.
Outline:	The pair with the ball try to keep possession of the ball as long as possible by means of positioning behind the defender, dribbling and dummying. The defender tries to get the ball by clever positioning.
Rules:	The two players keep passing until the defender touches it. He then changes positions with the player who last played the ball. Similarly if the ball goes out of play. Passes above head height are not permitted.
Possible variations:	1. The defender changes positions only if he manages to stop and control the ball. 2. If he only touches it the other two continue passing.
Remarks:	For less skilful players, the length of the play and intervals must be adapted to their stamina.

128   Three against Two

Purpose: Training for running off the ball and covering.
No. of players: 5. 3 v. 2.
Playing area: 20 × 20m.
Duration: 20 mins. maximum.
Outline: The three players in possession must keep the ball as long as possible by means of accurate interpassing, dribbling and dummying. The two defenders try to get the ball by clever positioning.
Rules: The three players keep possession until a defender touches it. When this occurs, the man who last played the ball changes with a defender. Similarly if the ball goes out of play or is passed above head height. Later, the players can change positions on a rota basis.
Possible variation: The defender changes positions only if he manages to stop and control the ball.
Remarks: Since the opportunities of passing in this game are more limited, good running off the ball becomes more important. The free man is allowed to signal as to where he wants the ball passed.

129 Four against Three

Purpose:	Training for running off the ball and covering.
No. of players:	7. 4 v. 3.
Playing area:	30 × 30m.
Duration:	30 mins. maximum.
Outline:	The four players in possession must try to keep the ball as long as possible by good running off the ball, avoiding the areas covered by the defence and intelligent running into free space in a game which reflects a fully competitive situation. The defenders try to win the ball by tactical positioning.
Rules:	The team of four keep the ball until it is touched by one of the defenders. If this occurs the two players concerned change positions. Similarly, if the ball goes out of play or if it is passed above head height, the attacker at fault switches with a defender, later perhaps on a rota basis.
Possible variation:	The defender changes position only if he manages to stop and control the ball.
Remarks:	In this game the defenders can shine: while one challenges the other two must cover both men and space.

130 Three Against Three With One Neutral Player

Purpose: Training for running off the ball and covering.
No. of players: 7. 3 v. 3 plus one neutral player.
Playing area: 30 × 30m.
Duration: 30 mins. maximum.
Outline: Players try to keep possession as long as they can by good interpassing. The neutral player always creates numerical superiority for the attack by playing with the team in possession. The three defenders try to intercept the ball by intelligent positioning.
Rules: The defenders become the attack if they manage to win the ball, if it goes out of play or is passed above head height. The game continues without interruption, the teams merely having switched functions.
Possible variation: The number of times the ball can be played may be limited to suit the skill of the players.
Remarks: For less skilful participants the playing of the ball can be linked to exercises of technique (e.g. passing off the "weak" foot etc.).

131 Five against Five without goals

Purpose:	Training for running off the ball and covering.
No. of players:	2 teams of 3–6.
Playing area:	Half a normal pitch.
Duration:	30 mins. maximum.
Outline:	The team with the ball tries to retain possession for as long as they can, the opposition tries to gain possession. If one team can keep the ball for a full minute they receive one point.
Rules:	One team starts the game by interpassing for as long as possible. The opposition must win the ball or wait until it goes out of play to gain possession. If the ball is retained for a full minute, the team may keep the ball and continue. Lofted passes are allowed.
Possible variation:	The points system can be altered to suit the teams concerned (e.g. one point for the fifth consecutive pass, for a good pass of 20m. or more, or for possession for a period greater or less than one minute).
Remarks:	The smaller the number of players, the more difficult retaining the ball becomes.

132   One-Goal Game

Purpose: Training for attack.
No. of players: 7. 4 v. 3.
Playing area: Half normal pitch including goal.
Duration: 30 mins. maximum.
Outline: Three attackers must play against four defence and score goals by going round or through them. The team who scores the most points is the winner.
Rules: The ball is given to the attack somewhere outside the penalty area. If they manage to get a shot at goal, either with the foot or the head, they receive one point; if a goal is scored they receive two. Only shots from within the penalty area count. If the defenders can intercept and kick the ball away over the centre-line they are awarded a point. The attack must then try to win the ball back.
Possible variation: Teams change over every five minutes. One defender remains.
Remarks: The game may also be played with 5 v. 4 or 6 v. 5.

133 Passing into the Gaps

Purpose:	Recognizing the gap.
No. of players:	10. 5 *v.* 5.
Playing area:	Double penalty area. One goal.
Duration:	20 mins. maximum.
Outline:	Teams must pass and move the ball until a gap appears in the defence through which they can shoot.
Rules:	If a goal is scored the successful team continues. Handling is not permitted, nor may any player cross the centre-line.
Possible variations:	1. Limit the number of times any player may play the ball. 2. Make it clear to the players whether they should use the inside of the foot only, or if they can use a full volley.
Remarks:	The size of the goal should be adapted to the players' abilities.

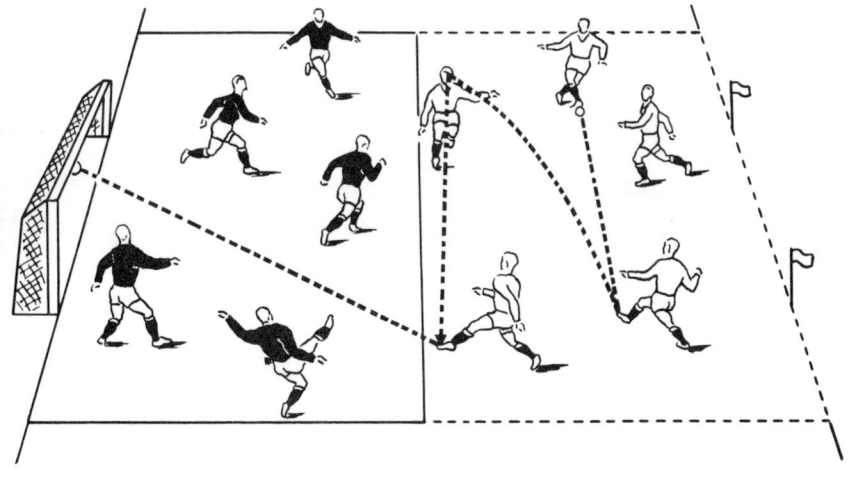

134 Three-Zone Game

Purpose:	Training for attack.
No. of players:	18. 8 v. 8 plus proper goalkeepers.
Playing area:	Full-size pitch. A line 25m. out from each goal-line, giving a central zone some 50m. wide.
Duration:	60 mins. maximum.
Outline:	One team mounts an attack, the other defends. The five forwards positioned in the centre-zone must quickly overcome the five opposing forwards so as to be able to penetrate the front-zone and so have only three defenders to beat to score a goal.
Rules:	Teams are composed of three defenders in the back-zone and five forwards in the centre-zone. The forwards may cross the line into their opponents' goal zone whereas the defence may not leave its zone, nor may their own forwards come back into it. No offside rule, but each team has its own goalkeeper.
Possible variation:	Switch the defenders with three of the attack after a given period of time.
Remarks:	The zones may be made smaller or larger to suit players' fitness and skill.

135 Five-Minute Game

Purpose:	Training the goal-attack.
No. of players:	2 teams of 4–6, 1 goalkeeper.
Playing area:	Half a normal pitch, with centre-line. Normal goal.
Duration:	6 periods of 5 mins. per team.
Outline:	One team tries to employ tactical variations to mount an attack and score, while the other defends.
Rules:	The game is started by the goalkeeper taking an impartial goal-kick into the far half, where the attackers are positioned. They manoeuvre themselves into a shooting position by intelligent positioning, dribbling along the wings, long crosses of the ball behind the defence, shooting through the defence and general combination play. The attack begins in the far half, where all the attackers must be before an attack begins. Defence and attack change positions every five minutes.
Possible variations:	1. Include additional defenders. 2. Employ further tactical variations.
Remarks:	Always arrange teams in their normal playing positions.

136 Long-Cross Game

Purpose: Training for the long cross.
No. of players: 2 teams of 8.
Playing area: Normal pitch with lines joining the sides of both penalty areas. Two diagonally opposite corners marked out.
Duration: 60 mins. maximum.
Outline: Three players defend and four attack in both of the side-zones. The attackers must pass the ball across to their team-mate in the marked corner to score one point.
Rules: A point is scored if the long cross lands directly in the corner. The other side receives the ball after each cross has been made, or if the attack loses the ball during the build-up. Balls in touch are thrown in. Free-kicks are awarded against any foul or against any player out of the playing area. The players positioned in the corners should be changed periodically.
Possible variations: 1. Increase the width of the zones to make the crosses easier.
2. To avoid inaction, one ball can be used on each side. This will necessitate having two referees.

137 Three-Team Game

Purpose:	Training for attack.
No. of players:	3 teams of 3–5.
Playing area:	Half normal pitch, two hockey goals.
Duration:	60 mins. maximum.
Outline:	One team attacks, trying to score goals, while the other two teams defend their goals and try to win the ball.
Rules:	The team in possession attack until a goal is scored or ball-possession is lost. If the ball is lost to the opposition the first team must take over the defence of the goal it had previously been attacking, while the other team now in possession attacks the other goal. Defending teams may not cross the centre-line. The last defender of any team may handle the ball in front of his goal. No offside rule.
Possible variations:	1. Teams with over five players should play with normal-size goals. 2. Vary the type of shot to be used.
Remarks:	The duration of this game should be adapted to the stamina of the players.

138 Shooting by Numbers

Purpose:	Training for running off the ball and covering.
No. of players:	2 teams of 3–5.
Playing area:	40 × 20m., two hockey goals.
Duration:	Until every player of one team has scored.
Outline:	Teams are numbered consecutively. Each player must score according to a prefixed sequence.
Rules:	One team starts the game by playing the ball between themselves so that their No. 1 can score. When No. 1 has scored, the team must manoeuvre No. 2 into a goal-scoring position and so on. The opposition continues the game if they win the ball, if the ball goes out of play, or if a foul is committed. No proper goalkeepers. The last defender of a team may handle the ball. No offside rule.
Possible variations:	1. Limit the number of times the ball may be played. 2. Fix which foot to be used for shooting.
Remarks:	This game is better suited to players of advanced skills.

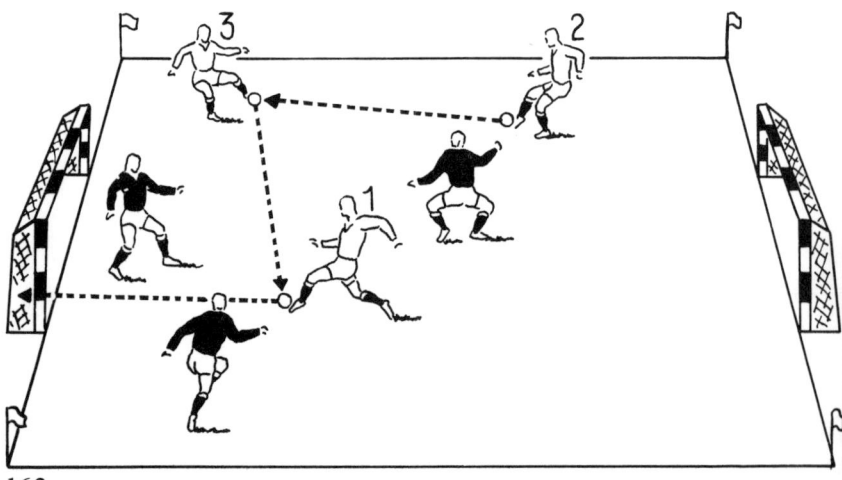

139   Upfield-Pass Game

Purpose:	Training for the upfield pass.
No. of players:	2 teams of 4–6. 1 proper goalkeeper.
Playing area:	Full pitch, including centre-line.
Duration:	30 mins. maximum.
Outline:	Both teams play in the half farthest from the occupied goal. The team in possession tries to retain the ball for as long as possible (one minute = one point). On the coach's whistle a long upfield pass into the free-zone is given by the team for one of its players to chase, from which he can shoot. The winner is the team who has the most passing points plus goals scored after the upfield pass.
Rules:	No player may cross the centre-line before the ball is passed into the other half. Ball possession changes if any pass is intercepted, if the shot is wide, or if a player loses control of the ball. No offside rule. Corners to be taken.
Possible variation:	After each attack play continues in the same half, the goalkeeper having to change ends.
Remarks:	The playing area should be reduced to crosswise over half the pitch for less advanced groups.

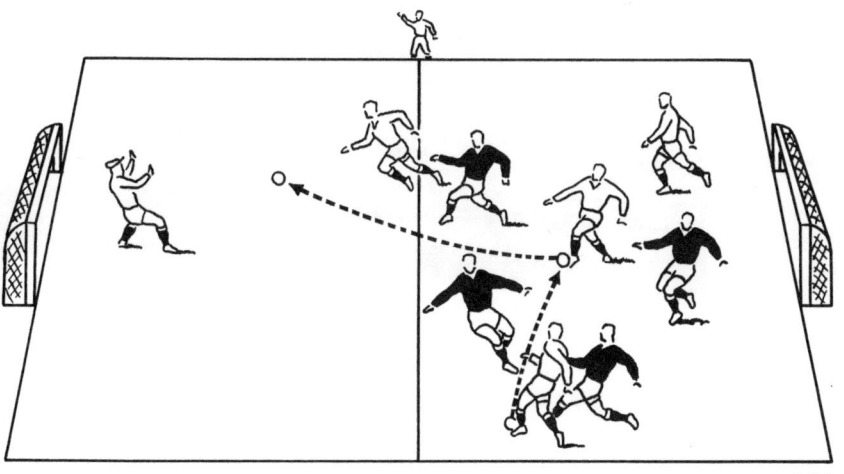

140 Shooting at Two Goals

Purpose:	Training for attack.
No. of players:	14, 6 *v.* 6, 2 goalkeepers.
Playing area:	Double the penalty area.
Duration:	30 mins. maximum.
Outline:	One team attacks, trying to score goals, the other defends and tries to win the ball.
Rules:	Defenders of both teams may not cross the centre-line. They become involved in attack in that they can take shots at the opposition goal from inside their own half. Similarly the forwards are restricted to the attacking half, so that three are always playing three in each half. A free-kick from the centre-line is awarded after any infringement. No offside. Back passes from forwards to their defence are allowed.
Possible variations:	1. One defender may cross into the other half to support the attack. 2. The size of the area can be increased by making the centre-line 20m. from the goals (i.e. length of area is 40m.).

141 Three against Two with Goals

Purpose: Training for attack.
No. of players: 2 teams of 5, with 2 goalkeepers.
Playing area: Full soccer pitch.
Duration: 30 mins. maximum.
Outline: Teams are made up of three attackers in one half and two defence in the other. Each team has one regular goalkeeper. The forwards pass the ball so that one of them can make a shot unchallenged. The defenders attempt to win the ball and pass it up to their attack.

Rules: The ball may cross the centre-line, but players may not. After each goal scored, balls out of play or interceptions, the other side continue the play. The goalie may pass either to the defence or up to the forwards. No offside rule.

Possible variations: 1. Teams of odd numbers, e.g. 4 *v.* 3 or 5 *v.* 4 are possible.
2. Game may be played across one half of the pitch with hockey goals and no goalkeepers.

142 Wingers Game

Purpose: Training for attack.
No. of players: 2 teams of 7–11.
Playing area: Full pitch. Additional goals 8–12m. wide placed at the sides 20–25m. from the goal-lines.
Duration: 40 mins. maximum.
Outline: The attacking team must play the ball through one of the outer goals before they can take a shot at the normal goal.
Rules: Only goals that have been scored via the outer goals count. This can be done in two ways: either a player can dribble the ball through the outer goal, or it can be passed through and then taken on by an inside forward.
Possible variation: Teams of less than seven should play across one half the pitch. Outer goals should be placed accordingly.
Remarks: The width of the outer goals should depend on the players' skills. The better the players, the narrower these goals should be.

143 Offside Trap

Purpose: Training for offside trap.
No. of players: 2 teams of 4–6, 1 goalkeeper.
Playing area: Half a normal pitch, including goal.
Duration: 60 mins. maximum.
Outline: One team starts attacking the goal from the centre-line while the other squad tries to lure the attackers offside by intelligent defence. One point is awarded to the attack for each goal scored, and to the defence for every man caught offside.
Rules: If the defence manages to win the ball, the attack must begin again. The offside ploys should be suited to the situation. Defensive manoeuvres can be man-to-man marking, covering space or combination play.
Possible variations: 1. The two teams change sides after a given time.
2. Change the number of players in attack or defence.
Remarks: A thorough explanation of the offside rule should precede this game.

144 Man-to-Man

Purpose:	Training for man-to-man marking.
No. of players:	2 teams of 4–8.
Playing area:	Half normal pitch, two hockey goals, centre-line.
Duration:	30 mins. maximum.
Outline:	The attackers of one team play in the opposing half, attempting to score, while the defence try to stop the other team scoring by means of thorough marking.
Rules:	The game is started by the defence passing the ball across the centre-line to the attack. These, in turn, are each closely marked by one defender. The defenders may tackle only their own man; help from other team members is not allowed. The opponents keep the ball if they beat their man in the tackle, after a goal, after fouls or if the ball goes out of play. No proper goalkeepers, no offside rule. The centre-line may not be crossed by any player. Handball is not permitted.
Possible variation:	Goalkeepers to be used, and defenders to be allowed shots at goal.
Remarks:	This game is particularly suitable for more highly skilled teams.

145 Triangular Goal Game

Purpose: Training covering of the goal.
No. of players: 2 teams of 3.
Playing area: Half normal pitch divided into two halves each containing three goalmouths (three flagposts placed in a triangle).
Duration: 60 mins. maximum.
Outline: One team attacks their opponents' half with the object of scoring through any side of the triangular goal, while one player of the other team each defends one side of the goal.
Rules: A goal is scored whenever the ball crosses any of the three goal-lines. A shot may be taken only from inside the attacking half. Each player is responsible for one goal-line. His teammates may not come to his aid by leaving their own goal untended. Ball possession changes after interceptions or saves, balls out of play, fouls and goals.
Possible variations: 1. No handball permitted.
2. All players can defend all goal-lines.
Remarks: The width of the goals and the length of the periods played should suit the stamina and ability of the players.

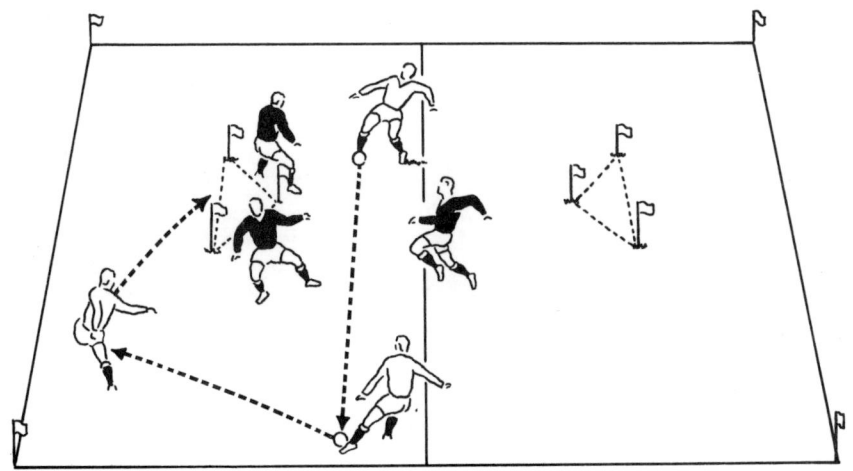

146 Positioning Game: Three Zones

Purpose: Training positional play.
No. of players: 2 teams of 9–11.
Playing area: Full pitch divided into three equal zones.
Duration: 40 mins. maximum.
Outline: Players take up their normal positions. In the end goal-zones, three attackers are against three defenders, in the centre-zone against the midfield players. Attacks are built up by passing the ball from one zone to another, with the object of scoring goals, or protecting the goal against opposition attacks.
Rules: The players may not leave their own zones. The game is started by the defence of one team passing the ball up into midfield. The ball may be passed only forwards out of the centre-zone. The final defender of each team may handle the ball within the penalty area. No offside rule.
Possible variations: 1. The ball may be passed directly right through the centre-zone.
2. The positions may be varied to suit team strategy, e.g. 4–3–3, 4–2–4, etc.
Remarks: If proper goalkeepers are used, the game becomes a fully competitive exercise.

147 Two-Ball Game

Purpose:	Training the peripheral vision.
No. of players:	2 teams of 5–7.
Playing area:	Half a normal pitch, without goals.
Duration:	30 mins. maximum.
Outline:	One team must retain possession of two balls for a given length of time. If the other team is in possession, they must tackle and harass their opponents.
Rules:	One team starts with both balls. One point is won if the balls are retained for two minutes. After this time is up the game continues until one or other ball is lost to the opponents, who are then also given the other one and start their two-minute stint. A team loses both balls if they commit a foul or a ball goes out of play.
Possible variations:	1. The time that both balls must be kept can be varied to suit the level of the players' skill (1–5 mins.). 2. Award points not on a time basis but according to the errors committed. Ball-possession changes after each error. 3. Teams of over seven players must use a full-size pitch.
Remarks:	Two referees should be used, one following each ball.

148 Rugby Ball Game

Purpose:	Training the reflexes.
No. of players:	2 teams of 5–11.
Playing area:	Half or full pitch depending on size of teams.
Duration:	45 mins. maximum.
Outline:	One team attacks the goal; the other defends and tries to intercept.
Rules:	Two teams play a normal game of soccer, but without any offside rule. The final defender of smaller teams may handle the ball.
Possible variations:	1. All variations of small-pitch soccer. 2. On a whistle from the coach, change the direction of play.
Remarks:	The value of this game obviously lies in the element of unpredictability, but this also increases the risk of injury and players should be conditioned to minimise the possibility.

149 Parallel Four-Goal Game

Purpose:	Improving peripheral vision.
No. of players:	2 teams of 6–11.
Playing area:	Normal pitch used sideways with two goals on either side. Centre-line.
Duration:	60 mins. maximum.
Outline:	One team attacks either one of their opponents' two goals, or defends its own goals.
Rules:	A goal is scored when the ball crosses either one of the goal-lines. Ball-possession changes after goals are scored, balls out of play, fouls, or fair tackles. No offside, but corners to be taken. There is also no kick-off from the centre, the ball being reintroduced into play by a goal-kick.
Possible variations:	1. All 22 players take part, the final defenders being permitted to handle the ball. 2. Two proper goalkeepers.
Remarks:	The further the two goals are set apart, the more successful changes of direction become.

150 Three-Goal Game

Purpose:	Improving peripheral vision.
No. of players:	2 teams of 8, with 1 neutral goalkeeper.
Playing area:	Half pitch, with normal goal plus two hockey goals at the sides.
Duration:	60 mins. maximum.
Outline:	One team attacks any one of the three goals, or defends them against the opposition.
Rules:	Goals may be scored in any one of the three goals. The goalkeeper is positioned in the larger goal; the smaller goals must be defended without use of the hands. If an attack is stopped, the defence must first attack one of the other two goals, to avoid "opportunist" goals.
Possible variations:	1. State whether a goal must be scored within a certain time or within a maximum number of passes. 2. On the whistle, the attack to switch to another goal. 3. Headed goals count double.
Remarks:	By limiting the rules either one of the teams may be given an advantage.

151   Goal with Three Goals in a Row

Purpose:	Training for peripheral vision.
No. of players:	2 teams of 4–6, one neutral goalkeeper.
Playing area:	Half the pitch, three goals each 1.50m. wide, with a 5m.-gap between them.
Duration:	40 mins. maximum.
Outline:	Teams try to kick the ball through any of the goals to score points. One goalkeeper tends all three goals.
Rules:	The game is started by the goalkeeper kicking the ball out impartially. Goals may be scored from either side, but not consecutively, i.e. without an intervening goal-kick. The game is stopped only for balls out of play, fouls, or an interception by the goalkeeper. A throw-in, free-kick or goal-kick respectively restarts the game.
Possible variation:	The width of the goals and the distance between them may be altered.
Remarks:	It is preferable to have two goalkeepers who relieve each other periodically.

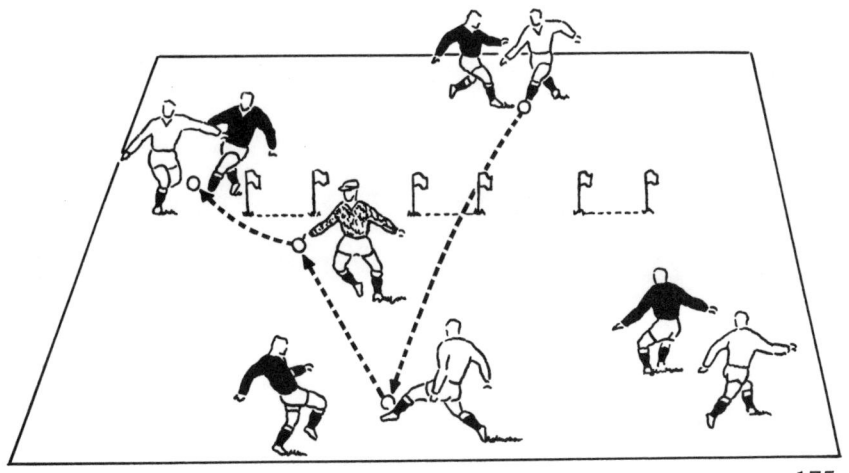

Supplementary games

152   Simple Basketball

Purpose:	Loosening up.
No. of players:	2 teams of 5.
Playing area:	26 × 14m. A basket with backboard 3.05m. high at either end. Front of the box 4.60m. from the baskets. Centre-circle.
Duration:	40 mins. maximum.
Outline:	One team tries to beat the opposition and throw the ball into the basket to score points. If the other team has the ball, the first team becomes the defence.
Rules:	To make this game effective as football training, it is not worth playing exactly to the proper rules of basketball. Practice has shown that handball rules are more appropriate, especially out of doors. Points to remember are: 1. Game is started by a bounce-up. 2. Fouls committed in the attacking half are penalised by a direct free shot, taken only by the player fouled. 3. A scoring shot made from open play counts two points, whereas a free shot after a foul counts only one.
Possible variations:	1. Increase or decrease number of players. 2. Allow no dribbling of the ball.
Remarks:	Pay particular attention to the no-bodily-contact rule.

153 Simple Handball

Purpose:	Loosening up.
No. of players:	2 teams of 7.
Playing area:	40 × 20m. Shooting circle of 6m. around both (hockey-sized) goals.
Duration:	60 mins. maximum.
Outline:	Both teams try to throw the ball into their opponents' net, or to protect their own goal.
Rules:	The ball may be played only with the hand. Following rules apply: 1. No more than three paces while holding the ball. 2. No player to enter shooting circle. 3. No obstruction allowed on any opponent. Minor fouls are penalised by a free throw, or if more serious by a penalty from 7m.
Possible variations:	1. Players may not run with or dribble the ball. 2. Increase or decrease the number of players.
Remarks:	The game may also be played with a rugby ball.

154 Medicine-ball Game

Purpose:	Loosening up.
No. of players:	2 teams of 4–6.
Playing area:	40 × 20m. No goals.
Duration:	30 mins. maximum.
Outline:	To win points, teams must retain possession of the ball for as long as possible. One point is given for every direct pass made successfully.
Rules:	The ball may be passed only by hand. Only direct passing allowed. Ball-possession changes if a pass is intercepted or the ball goes out of play. It is a good idea to have two referees, one following each team to count its points.
Possible variations:	1. Alter the method of scoring, e.g. one point for five good passes, or for retaining the ball one whole minute. 2. Vary the method of passing, e.g. only left- or right-handed, let the ball bounce once, only low passes, backward overhead passes, or even from between the legs.

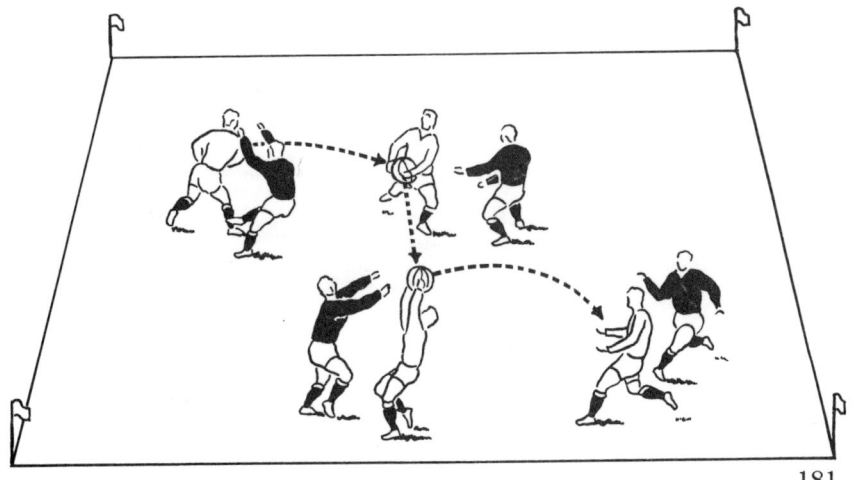

155 Fist-Tennis

Purpose: Loosening up.
No. of players: 1 v. 1.
Playing area: 8 × 4m., with a bench across the centre.
Duration: Best of three games of 21 points.
Outline: Scoring as in table-tennis. The ball to be used is a soccer ball (or volleyball) and the "bat" is the fist. The ball must be hit over the net into the other half and returned after having bounced once.

The first player to reach 21 points wins that game. The overall winner is the first to win two games. Change ends after ten points in a decider. Players each have five consecutive serves taken from behind the base-line. A fault occurs:

Rules:
1. If the service touches the net.
2. If the ball lands out of court.
3. If the ball bounces more than once.
4. If the ball is not played with the clenched fist.

Possible variation: Doubles, 2 v. 2.

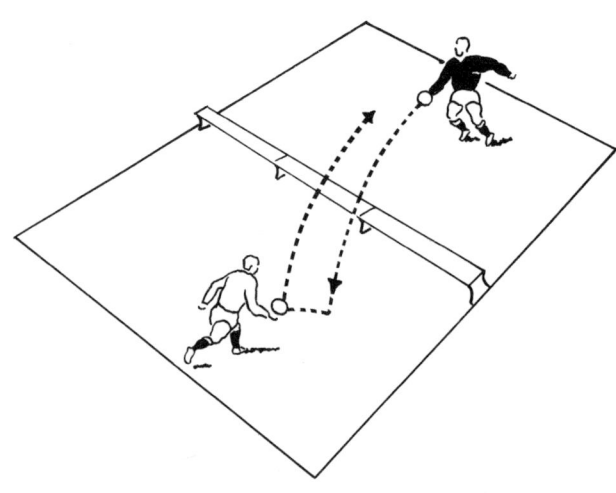

156 Simple Volleyball

Purpose:	Loosening up.
No. of players:	2 teams of 6.
Playing area:	Volleyball court. Net 2.40m. high.
Duration:	Best of three games of 15 points.
Outline:	Teams must knock the ball across the net with the flat of the hand and not let the ball bounce in their own court, which concedes a point. Points can be scored only on service.
Rules:	Services are made from behind the base-line after each fault. Players move round clockwise to take serve. In play, at least every third ball must be returned. If the team on serve makes a fault, the serve changes end. A fault occurs when the ball touches the ground, lands out of court, is played consecutively by the same man, is played by part of the body below the waist, or is held or caught. No player may touch the net or enter the opposition half.
Remarks:	The height of the net and/or the number of players may be altered.

157 Dry-Land Ice Hockey

Purpose:	Loosening up.
No. of players:	2 teams of 3–5.
Playing area:	Depending on size of gymnasium, but minimum 15 × 10m., with two indoor goals.
Duration:	20 mins. maximum.
Outline:	Each player is equipped with a stick or club about 40cm. long (a broom or spade handle will do). The ball is an old tennis ball or children's rubber ball. Teams try to manoeuvre the ball over their opponents' goal-line, for which they score a point, or to defend their own line.
Rules:	The game begins as in ice-hockey with a bully-off. The ball may be played or struck only with the stick. Handling or kicking the ball is forbidden. Only the goalkeeper may stop the ball with his hand but must restart play with his stick. Fouls are penalised by a free hit.
Possible variations:	1. The final defender of each team doubles as goalkeeper. 2. Draw a shooting circle: all shots from outside this area.